COOKING
FISH
&
GAME

Delicious Recipes
from Shore Lunches to Gourmet Dinners

THE HELICONIA PRESS

an Imprint of Fox Chapel Publishing
www.FoxChapelPublishing.com

© 2013 by Fox Chapel Publishing Company, Inc., 1970 Broad Street, East Petersburg, PA 17520.

Recipe selection, design, and book design © Fox Chapel Publishing.
Recipes and illustrations © G&R Publishing DBA CQ Products.

The photos on the following pages were provided by *Fotolia.com*:
fisherman © david hughes (cover), Magret de canard © L.Bouvier (cover), deer salami © tycoon101 (cover), Raw sea bass © Lilyana Vynogradova (cover), Hunter with dog © José 16 (page 4), The man in a boat © Kovalenko Inna and bow hunting whitetail © Dave Willman (page 9), Salmon Catch on Kijik Lake near Lake Clark National Park, Alaska © kevinbeasley (page 11), A lucky bass fisherman © sablin (page 15), Fish a catfish © margo555 (page 20), Trout being smoked © Foodlovers (page 29 and back cover), Fly fisherman holding a huge Brown Trout fish © mattjeppson (page 32), crappie fishing © Dave Willman (page 35), Barbecue Grill Salmon © Feng Yu (page 41 and cover), Walleye in hand © Piotr Wawrzyniuk (page 59), Happy fisherman holding a grouper © sablin (page 61), Hunter hunting the game, bird hunt © NanoStock (page 67), Deer roast with sauce © wjarek (page 71), Packing Meat © Michael Ireland (page 78), tasty beef jerky © Jiri Hera (page 85), Chesapeake Pup © Steve Udell (page 89), May I have this Dance © Steven Love (page 96), fagiano © fabiobag (page 98), Turkey Strut © Sidney Cromer (page 109), Deep Fat Fried Turkey © jlueders (page 111), Hunting Dog with a Mallard Duck © schlag (page 116), Eastern Cottontail Rabbit © visceralimage (page 122).

ISBN 978-1-896980-77-5

Library of Congress Cataloging-in-Publication Data

Cooking fish & game : the hungry sportsman's guide to preparing delicious meals from the great outdoors.
      pages cm
  Previously published as: I'm hooked!, c2007.
  Includes index.
  ISBN 978-1-896980-77-5
  1. Cooking (Fish) 2. Cooking (Game) I. Title: Cooking fish and game. II. Title: I'm hooked!
  TX747.C68 2013
  641.6'92--dc23
                              2012045852

To learn more about the other great books from Fox Chapel Publishing, or to find a retailer near you, call toll-free 800-457-9112 or visit us at *www.FoxChapelPublishing.com*.

Note to Authors: We are always looking for talented authors to write new books. Please send a brief letter describing your idea to Acquisition Editor, 1970 Broad Street, East Petersburg, PA 17520.

Printed in China
First printing

Because cooking raw meat and fish inherently includes the risk of infection and disease, this book cannot guarantee that creating the recipes in this book is safe for everyone. For this reason, this book is sold without warranties or guarantees of any kind, expressed or implied, and the publisher and the author disclaim any liability for any injuries, losses, or damages caused in any way by the content of this book or the reader's use of the recipes presented here. The publisher and the author urge all readers to thoroughly review each recipe and to understand the use of all the ingredients before beginning any recipe.

FRATERNAL ORDER OF SPORTSMAN CHEFS

VENI VENATUS VICI

CATCHING FOOD IS SERIOUS.*
COOKING IS THE ULTIMATE VICTORY.** HUNT TO COOK.

Cook proudly.

Cook generously.

Cook like a sportsman.

HERE'S THE FIELD GUIDE.

*…ly awesome. You know this. You're thinking about it right now.
**One you'll talk about for years. When your friends, family, and neighbors got to share in the bounty…and celebrated your skills.

TABLE OF CONTENTS

INTRODUCTION:
Catch It, Cook It, Eat It

If you've picked up this book, you know you are the ultimate hunter-gatherer. You fish, you hunt, you bring home the bacon. Armed with your fishing pole, rifle or crossbow (or perhaps all three), you rule the forest, the lake, the mountain. What you catch, you eat.

But before you eat it, YOU COOK IT.
That's right: COOK.

You are a hunter, so cook like a hunter. No oven mitts or Tupperware containers for you. You cook with a grill and a spatula (a big one, with a bottle opener in the handle). You cook with a pan over the open flame of a campfire (with your buddies and a cooler of beer at your side). You cook with pride, because you caught the food, and now you are going to enjoy it, and so is everyone else. In fact, when you set a crispy catfish or venison steak in front of them, they will applaud your skills.

You were THE HUNTER
and now you are THE COOK.

And this book is your guide to ultimate success in the kitchen. It contains recipes for anything you can catch—with a rifle or a fishing pole. Looking for a new hunting lodge favorite? Venison Barbecue in the Slow Cooker (page 75) can be prepped in fifteen minutes and then left in the slow cooker while you spend your day enjoying the great outdoors. Need to warm up after an early morning fishing trip? A bowl of Alaskan Salmon Chowder (page 45) ought to do the trick. And what about jerky? You will not be disappointed. Turn to page 86 for a collection of venison jerky marinades that will keep you full and happy until next year's deer season.

And while you're surveying the array of recipes for your tasting pleasure, make sure you check out the tips and sidebars that are, well, everywhere. They include fun facts, trivia and helpful information that will keep you on the right track to mastering the fine art of cooking delicious outdoor cuisine.

So pack up the tackle box, give your rifle a good polish and get your boots ready, because you're going to get dinner—like a hunter.

Hunting and fishing are activities that you can enjoy alone or with friends. They give you an opportunity to explore nature and triumph in the victory of a hard-earned catch.

★ ★ ★ ★ ★

AND REMEMBER:

EVERYONE REJOICES when the
HUNTER RETURNS.

Go catch them something
WORTHY OF
CELEBRATION.

★ ★ ★ ★ ★

COOKING FISH & GAME

CHAPTER 1

Fisherman's Paradise

Whether you're the angler in your family, the one back in the kitchen, or both, you probably think of the preparation of fish as the second part of a two-part process:

First you CATCH IT. Then you COOK IT.

Well, let the recipes in this chapter be the inspiration for your next fishing trip. Start by imagining a fresh-caught walleye grilling over red-hot coals, or a beer battered catfish sizzling in a pan. Maybe a sautéed bass drizzled with lemon dill butter will whet your appetite. Whatever you envision, keep it in mind the next time you grab your pole and head out for the water.

Because fishing is often a sport of patience, we know that you won't want to wait any longer than necessary to savor your catch after bringing it home. That's why we have done all the preparation for you by gathering the best flavor combinations, seasonings and marinades for the most popular freshwater fish in the United States.

Here, you will find delicious recipes for everything from salmon to crappie, plus a section for preparing fish from the sea. In addition, there are handy tips and information about each type of fish. So pack up your tackle box, go cast your line and enjoy the trip!

This salmon was caught on Kijik Lake, Alaska. Salmon meat tends to have a firmer consistency that is closer to red meat than other fish, like bass. For a hearty and healthy fish meal, go for salmon; for fish with a light flaky texture, try bass.

There are two types of bass:

BLACK BASS & TRUE BASS

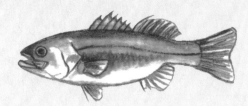

Largemouth Bass

Distribution Map: Largemouth Bass

Smallmouth Bass

Distribution Map: Smallmouth Bass

Black Bass are freshwater fish that are members of the sunfish family. The six species of Black Bass are: Largemouth, Smallmouth, Spotted, Guadalupe, Redeye and Suwannee. All of these species have long yellowish-greenish bodies. Of these species, the Largemouth and Smallmouth are the most popular game fish among American anglers.

Largemouth Bass are very strong and are known for their fighting ability. They live in lakes, ponds and rivers in the United States and Canada. Largemouths make a good meal and are a favorite fish of many anglers and eaters.

Smallmouth Bass are also incredibly strong for their size, as they weigh ½ pound to 4 pounds on average. They live in streams and large lakes in the United States as well as in parts of Canada, Europe and South America.

Spotted Bass, also known as Kentucky Bass, live in the southern regions of the United States. They are usually smaller than Smallmouths and are found in deep, clear reservoirs.

Guadalupe Bass live in streams in south-central Texas, while Redeye Bass live in streams in the Southeast. The Suwannee Bass can be found in the rivers of northern Florida.

Most True Bass species live in the ocean and are divided into two categories: Temperate Bass and Sea Bass. There are four species of True Bass in North America: White Bass, Yellow Bass, Striped Bass and White Perch. White and Yellow Bass live in freshwater but Striped Bass and White Perch live in the Atlantic Ocean. There are more than 370 species of Sea Bass living in the world's seas and oceans.

GRILLED BASS WITH FRESH SALSA

Makes: 4 to 8 servings   **Prep Time:** 25 minutes plus 1 hour marinating   **Cook Time:** 14 to 16 minutes

INGREDIENTS

- ½ C. cracked peppercorns
- ½ C. fresh lime juice
- 1 bunch fresh cilantro leaves, chopped
- ½ C. olive oil
- 2 (1- to 1½-lb.) whole bass fillets
- 1 lb. Roma tomatoes
- 1 to 2 jalapeño peppers, stemmed and seeded
- ½ yellow onion
- 6 to 8 cloves garlic
- 1 avocado
- ¼ C. olive oil
- 1 tsp. salt
- Pinch of pepper
- 2 bunches collard greens, washed

PREPARATION

In a large glass measuring cup, combine the peppercorns, lime juice, cilantro and ½ cup olive oil; whisk until well combined. Place the cleaned bass fillets in a 9 x 13" glass or ceramic baking dish. Pour the marinade over the bass. Cover and place the dish in the refrigerator for 1 hour.

Meanwhile, prepare the salsa. Preheat the oven broiler. Place the tomatoes, jalapeños and onion on a baking sheet. Tuck the garlic cloves under the other vegetables to prevent burning. Broil the vegetables for about 15 minutes or until they are well charred, turning every 2 to 3 minutes. Remove the baking sheet from the broiler and set the vegetables aside to cool.

Once the vegetables are cool, place them in a food processor; process until well combined. Pour the pureed mixture into a bowl. Peel and dice the avocado. Fold the avocado pieces and ¼ cup olive oil into the bowl; mix well. Season with salt and pepper; store in refrigerator.

Bring a large pot of lightly salted water to a boil over medium-high heat. Add the collard greens and blanch just until the water returns to a boil. Drain the pot and immediately fill with ice water. Drain again and remove the collard greens.

Preheat the grill to medium heat. Place the greens on a large baking sheet, overlapping to form two rectangles that are as long as each bass and twice as wide. Place each bass on one of the rectangles and wrap the greens over the fish so only the head and tail are exposed. Discard the marinade. Transfer the wrapped bass to the grill and cook for 7 to 8 minutes per side. Cut the fish into pieces and serve with salsa on the side.

"A bad day of fishing is better than a good day of work."

— AUTHOR UNKNOWN

SAUTÉED BASS IN LEMON DILL BUTTER

Makes: 2 to 4 servings   **Prep Time:** 10 minutes   **Cook Time:** 6 to 8 minutes

INGREDIENTS

- ➢ 1 lemon
- ➢ 1 (1-lb.) whole bass fillet
- ➢ ⅓ C. butter or margarine, softened
- ➢ 1 T. finely chopped green onion
- ➢ ½ tsp. dried dillweed
- ➢ ⅛ tsp. white pepper
- ➢ 2 T. flour
- ➢ ¼ tsp. paprika
- ➢ 1 T. olive oil
- ➢ Salt and pepper

PREPARATION

Cut the lemon into six wedges. Cut the cleaned bass fillet into two to four serving-size pieces and remove any skin. Squeeze the juice of two lemon wedges over both sides of each bass piece. Let stand for 5 minutes.

Meanwhile, in a small bowl, combine the butter, green onion, dillweed and white pepper. Grate the peel of the used lemon wedges and add the grated peel to the bowl. Mix everything until well combined. Set aside until ready to serve.

Using a paper towel, lightly pat the bass pieces dry. In a shallow pie plate, combine the flour and paprika. Dip each fish piece in the flour mixture, turning until lightly coated on both sides. Place the olive oil in a large non-stick skillet over medium-high heat. Once the oil is hot, sauté the fish for 3 to 4 minutes per side or until the fish turns opaque and flakes easily with a fork. Sprinkle the fish with salt and pepper to taste.

To serve, place each sautéed piece of bass on a serving plate. Garnish each serving with one lemon wedge. Spread 2 to 3 teaspoons of the lemon dill butter over each piece of fish and serve immediately.

★★★★ REEL 'EM IN ★★★★

BIG MOUTHS

Largemouth Bass feed often and a lot! They are greedy carnivores that have been known to eat minnows, sunfish, gizzard shad, insects, frogs and the occasional snake. Though it is difficult to consistently catch bass, they can be caught on a greater variety of baits and lures than practically any other fish. The most popular baits for catching bass are plastic worms, jigs, spinners, crank baits, minnow, crayfish, night crawlers and worms.

SOUTHERN-STYLE PAN-FRIED BASS

Makes: 8 servings **Prep Time:** 15 minutes plus 35 minutes soaking **Cook Time:** 6 to 10 minutes

INGREDIENTS

- 2 (2-lb.) whole bass fillets
- ½ C. flour
- ½ C. white, yellow or blue cornmeal
- ¼ C. finely minced green onions
- ½ tsp. sea salt
- ½ tsp. cayenne pepper
- 1 lemon
- 1 T. minced fresh parsley
- 1 C. milk
- 1 C. butter
- 6 sprigs fresh parsley

PREPARATION

Cut the bass into chunks or serving-size pieces and remove any skin. Rinse the fish pieces in cold water, then soak the pieces in a bowl of lightly salted water for 30 minutes.

Meanwhile, combine the flour, cornmeal, green onions, sea salt and cayenne pepper in a shallow pie plate; toss until well combined. Cut the lemon into six wedges and dust the center edge of each wedge with a little minced parsley; set aside. Add the remaining parsley to the flour mixture.

After 30 minutes, drain and rinse the fish. Pour the milk into a medium bowl. Place the fish pieces in the milk for 5 minutes. Next, dip each piece of fish in the flour mixture, pressing lightly and turning to coat both sides.

Place the butter in a large non-stick skillet over medium-high heat. Once the butter is melted, add the coated fish pieces and cook for 3 to 5 minutes per side or until the coating is golden. Remove the fried fish pieces from the skillet and place on paper towels to drain.

To serve, place the fish pieces on a serving dish. Garnish with the lemon wedges and fresh parsley sprigs.

Any fisherman would be happy to find this freshwater bass on the end of his line. Black Bass are the most popular game fish in the United States. An average of 40 to 45 percent of all anglers fish for Black Bass each year. The next most popular game fish is trout, which captures the attention of about 30 percent of the anglers in the United States.

The National Survey of Hunting, Fishing, and Wildlife-Associated Recreation.

BAKED BASS WITH AVOCADO SAUCE

Makes: 4 servings **Prep Time:** 15 minutes **Cook Time:** 14 minutes

INGREDIENTS

- 1 (1-lb.) whole bass fillet
- 1 large avocado
- ¼ C. milk
- 1 T. lime juice
- 1 clove garlic
- Dash of hot sauce
- 2 T. lemon juice
- 1 T. soy sauce
- 1 tsp. grated lemon peel
- 1 tsp. Dijon mustard
- ⅓ C. fine dry bread crumbs

PREPARATION

Preheat the oven to 450°F. Cut the bass fillet into four serving-size pieces.

Peel and coarsely chop the avocado. In a blender or food processor, combine the avocado pieces, milk, lime juice, garlic and hot sauce; process until smooth and chill in the refrigerator until ready to serve.

In a small bowl, combine the lemon juice, soy sauce, lemon peel and Dijon mustard; mix well. Place the bread crumbs in a shallow pie pan.

Lightly grease a baking sheet with non-stick cooking spray. Using a pastry brush, brush the mustard mixture evenly over both sides of each bass piece. Dip the pieces into the bread crumbs, turning to coat both sides. Place the coated fish pieces on the baking sheet. Bake for 7 minutes. Carefully turn each piece over and bake for an additional 7 minutes or until the fish flakes easily with a fork.

To serve, place each baked fish piece on a serving dish. Drizzle the avocado sauce over each serving.

★★★★ FISH TALES ★★★★

A SIXTH SENSE

In addition to sight, smell, taste, touch and hearing, bass have a sixth sense called the lateral line. Their lateral line is a series of sensitive nerve endings that extend from behind the gill to the tail on each side. The lateral line picks up underwater vibrations, even those as subtle as a swimming baitfish, allowing bass to survive in the murkiest waters.

SHRIMP-STUFFED BASS

Makes: 4 to 6 servings **Prep Time:** 15 minutes plus 45 minutes chilling **Cook Time:** 45 minutes

INGREDIENTS

- 1 (2-lb.) whole bass
- 1 tsp. salt
- 1 small onion
- 6 mushrooms
- 2 T. butter
- 2 T. minced fresh parsley
- 6 anchovies

- 10 small shrimp, peeled and cooked
- ⅓ C. dry bread crumbs
- 1 egg, slightly beaten
- Salt and pepper
- 1 T. lemon juice
- 2 strips bacon

- ½ C. butter, melted
- 1 medium onion
- 2 T. minced fresh parsley
- 1 C. white wine
- ¾ C. sour cream

PREPARATION

Remove the center bone from the bass, but do not cut it in half or behead. Wash the bass and pat dry with paper towels. Sprinkle salt all over the bass; place in the refrigerator for 45 minutes.

Preheat the oven to 450°F. To prepare the stuffing, mince the onion and chop the mushrooms. Melt the butter in a large skillet over medium-high heat. Add the onion, mushrooms and parsley; sauté until tender. Meanwhile, coarsely chop the anchovies and shrimp. Mix the anchovies, shrimp and bread crumbs into the skillet. Toss everything together and add the beaten egg. Cook for 2 additional minutes and remove from the heat.

Remove the fish from refrigerator, rinse and pat dry again with paper towels. Gently pry open the fish and sprinkle the inside with salt, pepper and lemon juice. Stuff the fish evenly with the shrimp mixture. Drape the bacon slices over the top of one side of the bass. Secure the stuffing and bacon in place with toothpicks.

Drizzle half of the melted butter in a 9 x 13" glass baking dish. Place the bass in the baking dish. Cut the remaining onion into slices. Place the onion slices and remaining 2 tablespoons of parsley over the fish. Drizzle the remaining butter over the fish and onion. Bake uncovered for 45 minutes, basting every 10 minutes with the white wine. During the last 10 minutes of baking time, add the sour cream to the baking dish around the fish. The fish is done when it flakes easily with a fork.

To serve, carefully place the fish on a serving dish. Remove the toothpicks. Spread the onions around the fish and drizzle with the sauce from the pan.

"Give me a fish and I will eat for a day.
Teach me to fish and I will eat for a lifetime."

— CHINESE PROVERB

FRESHWATER CATFISH of North America

There are more than 3,000 species of catfish. Some live in the ocean, but most live in freshwater. Catfish have whisker-looking barbels on their heads and do not have scales. Some catfish species have sharp spines and give off a poison once inside another animal's body.

There are about 45 catfish species that are native to North America. Some of the most popular species are Blue, Stonecat, Channel and Bullhead.

Blue Catfish, or Mississippi Catfish, are located primarily in the Mississippi River and the drainage of the river, as well as in a number of reservoirs and other rivers.

The Stonecat is usually found in warm clear water under logs and stones and grows to about 10" in length.

Channel Catfish thrive in small and large rivers, reservoirs, lakes and ponds. They are well-distributed throughout the United States. An average size for a Channel Catfish is 2 to 4 pounds, but they can weigh up to 50 pounds.

Bullhead Catfish are one of the easiest fish to catch, due to their persistence in taking the bait. The average bullhead caught weighs less than 1 pound and is about 12" in length.

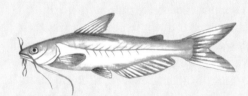

Blue Catfish

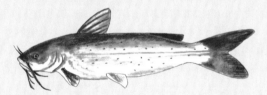

Channel Catfish

Stonecat

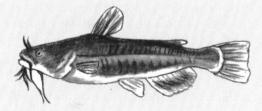

Bullhead Catfish

BLACKENED CATFISH

Makes: 2 to 4 servings   **Prep Time:** 10 minutes   **Cook Time:** 35 to 40 minutes

INGREDIENTS

- 2 tsp. cayenne pepper
- 2 tsp. lemon pepper
- 2 tsp. garlic powder
- 2 tsp. salt
- 2 tsp. pepper
- 1 lb. catfish fillets
- 2 T. butter or margarine, melted
- 1 C. Italian dressing

PREPARATION

Preheat the oven to 350°F. Lightly grease a medium baking dish and set aside. In a small bowl, combine the cayenne pepper, lemon pepper, garlic powder, salt and pepper; mix well.

Remove any skin from the cleaned catfish fillets. Using a pastry brush, brush both sides of the fillets with melted butter. Rub the seasoning mixture over both sides of each fillet.

Place a large heavy skillet over medium-high heat. Once the skillet is very hot, place the fillets in the skillet and cook for about 2 minutes on each side or until the outsides of the fillets are slightly blackened.

Arrange the blackened fillets in a single layer in the prepared baking dish. Lightly drizzle the Italian dressing over the fillets. Bake for 30 to 35 minutes or until the fish flakes easily with a fork.

To serve, place each baked fillet on a serving plate. If desired, pour the sauce from the baking dish over the fish on each plate.

★★★★ TACKLE BOX TRIVIA ★★★★

CATFISH GALORE

Catfish account for about half of the aquaculture in the United States. There are about 45 species of catfish that are native to North America, and the United States produces more than 300 million pounds of catfish (mostly Channel Catfish) on fish farms in Alabama, Arkansas and Mississippi.

CATFISH PARMESAN

Makes: 6 to 8 servings   **Prep Time:** 10 minutes   **Cook Time:** 40 minutes

INGREDIENTS

- ⅔ C. fresh grated Parmesan cheese
- ¼ C. flour
- ½ tsp. salt
- ¼ tsp. pepper
- 1 tsp. paprika
- 1 egg, beaten
- ¼ C. milk
- 1 lb. catfish fillets
- ¼ C. butter or margarine, melted
- ⅓ C. sliced almonds

PREPARATION

Preheat the oven to 350°F. Lightly grease a 9 x 13" baking dish. In a medium bowl, combine the Parmesan cheese, flour, salt, pepper and paprika; mix until well combined. In a separate bowl, combine the beaten egg and milk.

Remove any skin from the cleaned catfish fillets. Dip each catfish fillet first into the egg mixture and then into the flour mixture, turning to coat both sides. Arrange the coated catfish in the prepared baking dish.

Drizzle the melted butter over the catfish and sprinkle with the almonds. Bake for 35 to 40 minutes or until the fish flakes easily with a fork.

To serve, place each catfish fillet on a serving plate. Spoon some of the butter and almonds from the baking dish over each serving.

★★★★ FISH TALES ★★★★

CALLING ALL CATFISH

Most catfish are identified by their barbels, or cat-like whiskers. However, not all catfish have prominent barbels. The true way to identify a catfish is by certain features of the skull and swimbladder. And, unlike most fish, catfish do not have scales.

CAJUN CATFISH WRAPS

Makes: 4 servings   **Prep Time:** 15 minutes   **Cook Time:** about 10 minutes

INGREDIENTS

- 2 green onions
- 3½ C. finely shredded cabbage
- ¼ C. mayonnaise
- 1½ T. apple cider vinegar
- ½ tsp. sugar
- 3 T. chopped fresh cilantro
- 1 T. flour
- 1 T. paprika
- 1½ tsp. dried thyme
- 1½ tsp. dried oregano
- 1 tsp. garlic powder
- 1 tsp. pepper
- ½ tsp. salt
- ¼ tsp. cayenne pepper
- 1½ lbs. catfish pieces
- 1 T. butter
- 4 to 6 flour tortillas

PREPARATION

Finely chop the green onions. In a medium bowl, combine the green onions, cabbage, mayonnaise, apple cider vinegar, sugar and cilantro. Mix everything together until the ingredients are well combined and evenly coated with mayonnaise. Chill the coleslaw mixture in the refrigerator until ready to serve.

In a small bowl, combine the flour, paprika, thyme, oregano, garlic powder, pepper, salt and cayenne pepper. Rinse the catfish pieces and pat dry with paper towels. Dredge the catfish pieces in the seasoning mixture.

Place the butter in a large heavy skillet over medium heat. Once the butter is melted, sauté the catfish pieces for 5 minutes. Carefully turn them over and cook for 4 minutes on the other side.

Wrap the flour tortillas in damp paper towels. Microwave the wrapped tortillas for 30 seconds or until pliable. Divide the cooked catfish pieces onto the tortillas. Top each serving with about ¾ cup of the cole slaw mixture. Fold the sides in and wrap to enclose the fish and coleslaw.

"Three-fourths of the earth's surface is water and one-fourth is land. It is quite clear that the good Lord intended us to spend triple the amount of time fishing as taking care of the lawn."

— CHUCK CLARK

CRISPY CATFISH WITH HOMEMADE TARTAR SAUCE

Makes: 2 to 4 servings   **Prep Time:** 15 to 20 minutes   **Cook Time:** 20 minutes

INGREDIENTS

- ¼ C. butter or margarine
- ½ tsp. dried thyme
- ½ C. dry bread crumbs
- ½ tsp. lemon pepper
- 3 T. grated Parmesan cheese
- ½ tsp. dried oregano
- 1 lb. catfish fillets
- 1 C. mayonnaise
- 1 T. sweet pickle relish
- 1 T. minced onion
- 2 T. lemon juice
- Salt and pepper

PREPARATION

Preheat the oven to 425°F. Place the margarine in a 9 x 13" glass baking dish. Place the baking dish in the oven until the butter is melted.

Meanwhile, in a shallow pie plate, combine the thyme, bread crumbs, lemon pepper, Parmesan cheese and oregano; toss together until well combined.

Remove any skin from the cleaned catfish fillets. Rinse the fillets and pat dry. Once the butter is melted, remove the baking dish from the oven. Dip the catfish fillets in the butter, turning to coat both sides. Next, roll the catfish fillets in the seasoning mixture until evenly coated. Return the coated fish fillets to the same baking dish. Bake for 20 minutes or until the fish flakes easily with a fork.

Meanwhile, prepare the tartar sauce. In a small bowl, combine the mayonnaise, pickle relish, onion and lemon juice. Season with salt and pepper to taste; mix until well combined.

To serve, place the baked catfish on a serving dish. Serve with tartar sauce on the side.

★★★★ SPORTSMAN COOKING ★★★★

QUICK AS A CAT

Grilling, baking, pan frying and broiling are popular ways to prepare catfish. But did you know catfish can also be prepared in the microwave? To microwave one catfish fillet, cut the fillet in half so the thick center portions are to the outside. Place the fillet in a microwave-safe dish that has been coated with non-stick cooking spray. Microwave on high for 6 to 8 minutes.

SEASONED CATFISH CAKES

Makes: 4 servings   **Prep Time:** 25 minutes   **Cook Time:** 4 minutes

INGREDIENTS

- 1 lb. catfish fillets
- 1 medium onion
- 1 tsp. prepared yellow mustard
- 1 T. mayonnaise
- ½ tsp. Old Bay seasoning
- 2½ C. coarsely crushed round butter crackers
- 1 egg
- 1 C. vegetable oil

PREPARATION

Place the catfish fillets in a large saucepan. Fill with enough water to cover the fish and place over medium-high heat. Bring the water to a boil and cook the fish until it flakes easily with a fork. Drain the water from the saucepan and transfer the cooked fish to a medium bowl. Break up the fish into small pieces with a fork and remove any skin.

Chop the onion. Add the onion, yellow mustard, mayonnaise, Old Bay seasoning, cracker crumbs and egg to the bowl with the flaked fish. Mix everything together until evenly blended.

Place the oil in a large skillet over medium-high heat. Meanwhile, form the fish mixture into six to eight patties of even thickness. Once the oil is hot, fry the patties in the skillet for 2 to 4 minutes on each side or until lightly browned. Remove the patties to paper towels to drain. Serve hot with tartar sauce or cocktail sauce on the side.

"Nothing makes a fish bigger than almost being caught."

— AUTHOR UNKNOWN

★★★★ REEL 'EM IN ★★★★

THEY'LL EAT ANYTHING

Some common catfish baits are crawfish, shrimp, cut fish bait, clams, worms and minnows. However, catfish have been caught with many types of miscellaneous bait, including: bread dough, salmon eggs, smoked salmon, corn, hot dogs, bologna, salami, green peas, plastic worms, grubs and orange cheese. Some anglers believe catfish will nibble at almost any animal, vegetable or mineral you put on your hook.

FRESHWATER & SALTWATER TROUT

Trout are closely related to salmon, whitefish and char. Most trout species live in freshwater streams and lakes.

Some of the most popular types of trout are Rainbow, Steelhead, Cutthroat, Brown, Brook and Lake. All trout have streamlined bodies with small scales and strong teeth.

Rainbow Trout are native to tributaries of the Pacific Ocean in North America and Asia but can also be found in other parts of the United States, particularly northern states. The ocean-dwelling form of the Rainbow Trout is known as Steelhead Trout. Steelheads stay in the ocean for 1 to 4 years but return to fresh water to spawn. Rainbow Trout range from 12" to 36" in length and Steelheads grow from 20" to 48".

The two subspecies of Cutthroat are the Coastal Cutthroat and the Westslope Cutthroat, and it can often be difficult to tell the two apart. The average cutthroat is 12" to 15" in length and can weigh between ½ pound to 17 pounds. Cutthroats have a short, conical head with a pointed snout and well-developed teeth. These fish get their name from the yellow, orange or red lines in the skin folds on both sides of their lower jaws.

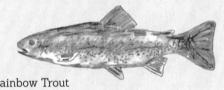

Rainbow Trout

Brook Trout

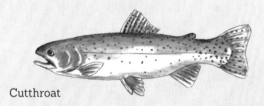

Cutthroat

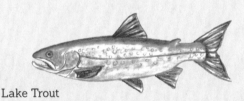

Lake Trout

Brown Trout

Brown Trout are medium-sized fish that can grow up to 40 pounds, but most Brown Trout found in smaller rivers weigh 2 pounds or less. The spawning behavior of Brown Trout is similar to that of the Atlantic Salmon. A typical female will produce 900 eggs per pound of body weight.

While some Brook Trout live in the sea, most are native to small streams, creeks, lakes and spring ponds. Though it is commonly considered a trout, the Brook Trout is actually a char, along with Lake Trout.

Lake Trout are slow-growing fish that live primarily in lakes of northern Canada, Alaska and the northeastern United States. Most Lake Trout weigh less than 5 pounds, but they can weigh up to 20 pounds.

FISHING TRIP PACKING

If you are investing the time and money to go on an extended fishing trip, you should also take the time to plan ahead and pack well. While it might take some extra forethought, packing well before a trip guarantees you more time out on the water.

INVEST IN THE RIGHT LUGGAGE. Luggage designed specifically for fishing trips has a leg up on the suitcase you already have in your closet. Angler's luggage usually has specially designed pockets for your fishing rods to keep them safe and secure during travel. Using luggage like this means you can pack up your rods and leave behind the heavy and unwieldy aluminum tubes that came with the rods when you purchased them.

KNOW WHAT TO PACK. To know what to pack, you have to know about your destination and what your travel companions are bringing. If waders are available for loan, you don't need to pack them. If there's a beer distributor nearby, you can purchase a case when you get there. If your buddy is bringing his extra rods and is willing to share, you can leave yours at home. Know what you need and don't need so you can pack accordingly.

PACK FOR THE BOAT NOW. Because you're already thinking ahead to your destination, you might as well think ahead to the boat as well. Pull together all the gear you'll need when you're actually out on the water and pack it in a separate bag. Now, when you're ready to fish, all you have to do is grab the bag and go.

BAKED STUFFED TROUT

Makes: 8 servings   **Prep Time:** 30 minutes   **Cook Time:** 20 minutes

INGREDIENTS

- 8 (½- to 1-lb.) whole trout
- 8 slices stale bread
- 1 small onion
- 2 stalks celery
- ¼ C. butter or margarine
- 2 tsp. minced garlic
- 1 C. chicken broth
- 2 tsp. chopped fresh thyme
- 2 tsp. salt
- 1 tsp. pepper
- ½ tsp. hot pepper sauce
- ½ C. butter or margarine, melted
- 3 T. lemon juice

PREPARATION

Gut the trout, removing the heads and tails. Rinse the inside and outside of the fish and pat dry with paper towels. Cut or tear the stale bread into 1" pieces and place in a medium bowl; set aside. Chop the onion and dice the celery.

Preheat the oven to 350°F. Place the butter in a large skillet over medium heat. Once the butter is melted, add the onion, celery and garlic; sauté until the onions just begin to turn brown.

Add the chicken broth, thyme, salt and pepper to the onion mixture in the skillet; stir well. Add the hot pepper sauce and simmer for 2 to 3 minutes. Pour the mixture over the bread pieces in the bowl and toss until completely moistened. Divide the stuffing into eight portions. Stuff each trout evenly with one of the stuffing portions and secure with toothpicks. Place the stuffed trout in two 9 x 13" glass baking dishes. Bake for 20 minutes or until the fish flakes easily with a fork.

Meanwhile, combine the melted butter and lemon juice in a small bowl. To serve, transfer the baked trout to a serving dish and carefully remove the toothpicks. Drizzle the stuffed trout with the melted butter mixture and serve.

"Even if you've been fishing for three hours and haven't gotten anything except poison ivy and sunburn, you're still better off than the worm."

— AUTHOR UNKNOWN

ALMOND TROUT

Makes: 2 servings **Prep Time:** 15 minutes **Cook Time:** 15 minutes

INGREDIENTS

- 2 (½- to 1-lb.) trout, dressed
- Salt and pepper
- ¼ C. flour
- 4 T. butter or margarine, divided
- ½ C. blanched slivered almonds
- 2 T. lemon juice
- 1 lemon
- 1 T. chopped fresh parsley

PREPARATION

Rinse the trout and pat dry with paper towels. Season the inside and outside of the trout with salt and pepper to taste. Place the flour in a large pie plate and dredge the trout in the flour.

Place 2 tablespoons of butter in a large skillet over high heat. Once the butter is melted, add the trout to the skillet and cook, turning once, until browned on both sides. Reduce the heat to medium and continue to cook for about 5 minutes on each side or until the fish flakes easily with a fork. Remove the trout to a serving plate and keep warm.

Quickly wipe out the skillet with a wet paper towel and add 2 more tablespoons of butter. Place the skillet over medium heat just until the butter begins to brown. Add the almonds and sauté until lightly brown. Drizzle the butter sauce and almonds over the fish. Sprinkle the lemon juice lightly over the fish.

Cut the lemon into slices. Garnish the fish with the lemon slices and chopped fresh parsley. Serve immediately.

★★★★ **FISH TALES** ★★★★

SOME LIKE IT COLD

Trout are considered a cold water fish and require low water temperatures and high dissolved oxygen levels in order to survive. The optimal temperature for trout habitat is between 50° and 65°F in water with healthy aquaculture to ensure adequate oxygenation. Trout begin to show signs of stress at 70°F and will most likely die in 80°F water.

BARBECUE GRILLED OR BROILED TROUT

Makes: 4 to 6 servings   **Prep Time:** 15 minutes plus 30 minutes marinating   **Cook Time:** 10 to 16 minutes

INGREDIENTS

- ➢ 4 to 6 (½- to 1-lb.) whole trout
- ➢ 2 T. butter or margarine
- ➢ 1 clove garlic
- ➢ ½ small onion
- ➢ ½ small green bell pepper
- ➢ 1 (8-oz.) can tomato sauce
- ➢ 2 T. lemon juice
- ➢ 1 T. Worcestershire sauce
- ➢ 1 T. brown sugar
- ➢ ½ tsp. chili powder
- ➢ 2 T. lemon juice

PREPARATION

Cut the cleaned and scaled trout into serving-size portions and place them in a single layer in a 9 x 13" glass baking dish.

Place the butter in a large skillet over medium-high heat. Mince the garlic and chop the onion and green pepper. Once the butter is melted, sauté the garlic, onion and green pepper until the onion is softened. Stir in the tomato sauce, lemon juice, Worcestershire sauce, brown sugar and chili powder. Bring the mixture to a simmer for 5 minutes, stirring occasionally. Remove from heat and let cool.

Once cooled, pour the sauce over the fish in the baking dish. Cover and place the baking dish in the refrigerator for 30 minutes to marinate, turning the fish after 15 minutes.

Preheat an outdoor grill or the oven broiler to high heat. Remove the fish from the marinade and place in well-greased, hinged grill baskets or on broiler racks. Transfer the marinade to a medium saucepan over medium-high heat. Bring the marinade to a rolling boil for 5 minutes and remove from heat. Grill or broil the fish about 4" from the heat for 5 to 8 minutes. Baste the fish with the boiled marinade. Turn the fish over and grill or broil for an additional 5 to 8 minutes or until the fish flakes easily with a fork.

To serve, transfer the grilled or broiled fish to a serving dish and sprinkle with 2 tablespoons of lemon juice.

"Calling fly-fishing a hobby is like calling brain surgery a job."

AUTHOR UNKNOWN

Diners are sure to enjoy this group of trout being smoked for dinner. Fish like salmon and trout contain a good deal of oil, making them perfect for smoking, as they come out with a great smoked flavor and texture. Fish that have less oil can become dried out and tough during smoking.

SWISS BAKED WHOLE TROUT

Makes: 6 servings   **Prep Time:** 10 to 15 minutes   **Cook Time:** 15 minutes

INGREDIENTS

- 6 (½- to 1-lb.) whole trout
- 1 onion
- 3 oz. fresh mushrooms
- 1 tsp. chopped fresh parsley
- Salt and pepper
- ½ tsp. dried tarragon
- 2 T. butter or margarine, melted
- 4 egg yolks
- 3 T. brandy
- ½ tsp. salt
- ⅛ tsp. white pepper
- ½ C. dry bread crumbs
- ½ C. shredded Swiss cheese
- ⅛ tsp. paprika

PREPARATION

Gut the trout but leave the heads and tails intact.

Preheat the oven to 400°F. Lightly grease a 9 x 13" glass baking dish. Finely chop the onion and mushrooms. Place the onion and mushrooms in an even layer across the bottom of the baking dish. Sprinkle the parsley, salt and pepper over the onion and mushrooms.

Arrange the trout over the vegetables. Sprinkle the tarragon over the fish and drizzle with the melted butter. Cover the baking dish with aluminum foil. Bake for 10 minutes.

Meanwhile, in a small bowl, combine the egg yolks, brandy, salt and white pepper. Remove the foil from the baking dish and pour the egg mixture evenly over the fish. Sprinkle the bread crumbs, Swiss cheese and paprika over the trout. Return the baking dish to the oven for 5 minutes or until the fish flakes easily with a fork and the bread crumbs are lightly browned.

To serve, place one whole baked trout on each serving plate. Drizzle the sauce, onions and mushrooms from the pan over each serving.

★★★★ TACKLE BOX TRIVIA ★★★★

IT'S ALL IN THE FAMILY

This table shows the average length, weight and lifespan of fish in the trout family.

TROUT	LENGTH	WEIGHT	LIFESPAN
Brook	10–12"	4 to 6 lbs.	8 years
Golden	10–14"	1 to 7 lbs.	7 to 12 years
Cutthroat	12–15"	½ to 17 lbs.	12 years
Brown	14–24"	2½ to 10 lbs.	12 years
Rainbow	20–23"	4 to 8 lbs.	3 to 8 years
Lake	20–24"	2 to 6 lbs., up to 20 lbs.	up to 20 years

PAN-FRIED TROUT IN PECAN SAUCE

Makes: 4 servings   **Prep Time:** 15 minutes   **Cook Time:** 4 to 8 minutes

INGREDIENTS

- ½ C. pecan halves
- 2 green onions
- 1 clove garlic
- ¼ C. butter or margarine, softened
- 1 tsp. lemon juice
- ⅛ tsp. grated lemon peel
- ½ tsp. hot pepper sauce
- 4 (½-lb.) trout fillets
- ¼ C. flour
- 2 T. finely ground pecans
- ¾ tsp. salt
- ¼ tsp. white pepper
- Pinch of cayenne pepper
- 2 T. vegetable oil
- ¼ C. butter or margarine

PREPARATION

Begin by preparing the pecan sauce. Preheat the oven to 350°F. Arrange the pecan halves in an even layer on a baking sheet. Bake the pecans for 8 minutes or until lightly browned. Coarsely chop the green onions and mince the garlic. In a blender, combine the toasted pecans, green onions, garlic, ¼ cup of butter, lemon juice, lemon peel and hot pepper sauce. Process on high until well blended and smooth; set aside.

Rinse the trout fillets and pat dry with paper towels. In a medium bowl, combine the flour, ground pecans, salt, white pepper and cayenne pepper. Dredge the fillets in the flour mixture, turning to coat both sides.

Meanwhile, place the vegetable oil and ¼ cup of butter in a large skillet over medium-high heat. Once the butter is melted, place the trout fillets in the skillet and fry for 2 to 4 minutes per side or until the coating is golden brown. Remove the trout to paper towels to drain.

To serve, place the fried trout fillets on a serving dish and spread a generous 2 tablespoons of the pecan sauce over each fillet.

"Trout that doesn't think two jumps and several runs ahead of the average fisherman is mighty apt to get fried."

BEATRICE COOK, *Till Fish Do Us Part*

ASIAN GRILLED TROUT

Makes: 4 servings **Prep Time:** 10 minutes **Cook Time:** 4 to 8 minutes

INGREDIENTS

- ¼ C. safflower oil
- 1 T. grated gingerroot
- ½ tsp. crushed red pepper flakes
- 2 T. lime juice
- 1 tsp. grated lime peel
- 4 (½-lb.) trout fillets
- Salt and pepper

PREPARATION

Place the safflower oil in a small saucepan over medium-high heat. Once the oil is hot, sauté the gingerroot until just lightly browned and fragrant. Remove the saucepan from the heat and stir in the crushed red pepper flakes. When the oil cools completely, gradually whisk in the lime juice and lime peel. Mix well and set aside.

Preheat the grill to high heat and lightly oil the grate. Season the trout fillets with salt and pepper to taste. Once the grill is hot, grill the trout, flesh side down, for 2 to 4 minutes. Gently turn the fillets over and grill for 2 to 4 additional minutes or until the fish turns opaque.

To serve, immediately transfer the grilled trout to serving plates. Drizzle the lime and ginger mixture over each fillet and serve.

The beautiful coloring of this fish marks it as a Brown Trout. Brown Trout have earned the reputation of being one of the smartest and most difficult fish to catch. Brown Trout are nocturnal and your best chance of catching one is at dusk or dark, but be ready for a tug-of-war, as they prefer to stay under the water and tug out the fight.

CRAPPIE & BLUEGILL

Crappie and Bluegill are both members of the sunfish family and both are popular game fish.

The two types of crappies are White Crappie and Black Crappie

White Crappie are native throughout the eastern half of Canada and the United States. They prefer the slow-moving or turbid water of a small creek or large lake.

Black Crappie have been so widely transplanted that it is hard to determine their range. Populations of the Black Crappie have been found in all of the lower 48 states. Black Crappie tend to prefer clearer water than White Crappie.

Bluegill are sometimes referred to as bream, brim or coppernose. They are native to North America and can be found from Canada to northern Mexico. Bluegill are easily identified by the blue or black tip on the gills in the "ear" areas. However, their name comes from the bright blue edging that is visible on their gill rakers. Bluegill grow to a maximum of 16" in length.

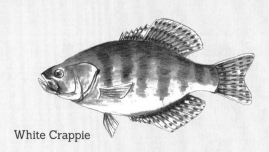
White Crappie

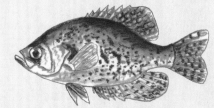
Black Crappie

Bluegill

"Even eminent chartered accountants are known, in their capacity as fishermen, blissfully to ignore differences between seven and ten inches, half a pound and two pounds, three fish and a dozen fish."

WILLIAM SHERWOOD FOX, *Silken Lines and Silver Hook*

LEMON PEPPER CRAPPIE

Makes: 4 servings **Prep Time:** 15 minutes plus 30 minutes marinating **Cook Time:** 6 to 10 minutes

INGREDIENTS

- ➤ 4 crappie fillets
- ➤ 1 (12-oz.) bottle lemon pepper marinade
- ➤ 1 C. dry bread crumbs
- ➤ ½ tsp. seasoned salt
- ➤ ½ tsp. lemon pepper
- ➤ 2 T. vegetable oil
- ➤ 2 T. butter or margarine
- ➤ ⅓ C. light cream or half-and-half
- ➤ 1 T. grated lemon peel
- ➤ ⅓ C. sliced almonds

PREPARATION

Place the crappie fillets in a resealable plastic bag. Pour the lemon pepper marinade over the fish and seal the bag. Place the bag flat in the refrigerator for 30 minutes to marinate. Turn the bag over after 15 minutes.

Meanwhile, in a pie plate, combine the bread crumbs, seasoned salt and lemon pepper; mix well. After 30 minutes, remove the crappie fillets from the marinade and roll in the bread crumb mixture until evenly coated, turning to coat both sides. Discard the marinade.

Place the vegetable oil and butter in a large skillet over medium-high heat. Once the butter is melted, add the coated crappie fillets and cook for 3 to 5 minutes on each side, or until the fish flakes easily with a fork and the coating is golden brown. Remove the fish to a serving dish and keep warm.

Add the cream and lemon peel to the same skillet over medium heat; bring to a boil, stirring constantly, until slightly thickened. Spoon the sauce over the fillets and sprinkle with the sliced almonds. If desired, toast the almonds before sprinkling over the fish by placing them in an even layer on a baking sheet in a 350°F oven for 8 minutes or until golden brown.

★★★★ SPORTSMAN COOKING ★★★★

FAST FOOD

Fish is the ultimate fast food. Most fish can be cooked within 10 minutes for every inch of thickness. For frozen unthawed fish, double the cooking time to 20 minutes for every inch of thickness. Most fish is done being cooked when it turns opaque, meaning that the meat of the fish is no longer clear and no light can pass through it. Opaque fish looks dull-white instead of shiny.

YOGURT BAKED CRAPPIE

Makes: 8 to 10 servings   **Prep Time:** 10 to 15 minutes   **Cook Time:** 15 to 20 minutes

INGREDIENTS

- 1 C. plain yogurt, chilled
- 1 C. flour
- 1 C. dry bread crumbs
- 1 T. Old Bay seasoning
- ½ tsp. Creole seasoning
- ½ tsp. dried basil
- ½ tsp. dried thyme
- ½ tsp. garlic powder
- ½ tsp. dried oregano
- ¼ tsp. pepper
- ⅛ tsp. cayenne pepper
- 8 to 10 crappie fillets
- 1 hard-boiled egg
- 1 C. mayonnaise
- ⅓ C. sweet pickle relish
- 1 T. minced capers
- Dash of Worcestershire sauce
- Dash of hot pepper sauce
- Salt and white pepper

PREPARATION

Preheat the oven to 400°F. Lightly coat a baking sheet with non-stick cooking spray.

Place the plain yogurt in a medium bowl. In a separate bowl, combine the flour, bread crumbs, Old Bay seasoning, Creole seasoning, basil, thyme, garlic powder, oregano, pepper and cayenne pepper; mix until well combined.

Dip the crappie fillets in the yogurt and then place them in the seasoning mixture, turning to coat both sides. Place each coated crappie fillet on the prepared baking sheet. Bake for 15 to 20 minutes or until the fish flakes easily with a fork.

Meanwhile, prepare the tartar sauce. Peel and chop the hard-boiled egg. In a small bowl, combine the chopped egg, mayonnaise, pickle relish, capers, Worcestershire sauce and hot pepper sauce. Season with salt and white pepper to taste; mix until well combined. Place the baked crappie on a serving dish and serve with tartar sauce on the side.

This triumphant fisherman has pulled in a Black Crappie. When fishing for Crappie, it is important to remember that their mouths are smaller than those of many other fish species. Because of this, switch to small lures and hooks when fishing for Crappie.

STIR-FRY CRAPPIE

Makes: 4 to 6 servings   **Prep Time:** 10 to 15 minutes   **Cook Time:** 6 to 10 minutes

INGREDIENTS

- 2 to 3 stalks celery
- 1 green bell pepper
- 3 green onions
- 6 to 8 fresh mushrooms
- 4 to 6 crappie fillets
- 2 T. vegetable oil
- 1 T. cornstarch
- ¼ tsp. garlic powder
- 2 tsp. chicken bouillon granules
- ¼ C. soy sauce
- 1½ C. chicken broth
- Hot cooked rice

PREPARATION

Cut the celery stalks diagonally into ¼" slices. Cut the green pepper into ¼" strips. Chop the green onions and slice the mushrooms. Cut the crappie fillets into 1½" strips.

Place the vegetable oil in a large heavy skillet or wok over medium-high heat. Once the oil is hot, sauté the crappie strips, celery, green pepper strips, green onions and mushrooms for 3 minutes, stirring constantly.

In a small bowl, combine the cornstarch, garlic powder and chicken bouillon granules. Add the cornstarch mixture, soy sauce and chicken broth to the skillet. Bring to a boil for 3 minutes or until the sauce is thickened and hot.

Place a bed of hot cooked rice on each serving plate and spoon some of the stir-fry crappie, vegetables and sauce over the rice.

★★★★ TACKLE BOX TRIVIA ★★★★

NOT SO BLACK & WHITE

It is often difficult to tell a Black Crappie from a White Crappie. You cannot rely on color alone as the colors vary widely depending on the clarity of the water, the season and the spawning conditions. One way to tell the difference is by counting the spiny dorsal rays; a Black Crappie will have seven or eight while a White Crappie will have just five or six. Also, the distance from the eye to the front of the dorsal fin on a White Crappie is greater than the distance along the base of the dorsal fin. In comparison, these two measurements are nearly equal on a Black Crappie.

SPINACH & CRAPPIE CASSEROLE

Makes: 4 to 6 servings   **Prep Time:** 20 minutes   **Cook Time:** 30 to 40 minutes

INGREDIENTS

- 3 stalks celery
- 1 small onion
- 2 cloves garlic
- 2 T. olive oil
- 1 T. butter or margarine
- 1½ C. chopped fresh spinach
- 1 (7-oz.) can mushrooms
- 1½ lbs. crappie or bluegill pieces
- ½ C. soft bread crumbs
- 2 eggs, beaten
- Salt and pepper
- Pinch of dried dillweed
- ⅓ C. crumbled feta cheese
- Salt and pepper
- Pinch of paprika
- ½ C. soft bread crumbs
- 3 T. butter, melted
- Dash of lemon juice

PREPARATION

Chop the celery and onion. Mince the garlic. Place the olive oil and 1 tablespoon of butter in a large skillet over medium-high heat. Add the celery, onion and garlic; sauté until tender. Add the spinach and continue to cook and stir until the spinach wilts. Drain the mushrooms and add to the skillet, stirring until heated through. Set aside and cover to keep warm.

Lightly grease a 9" square glass baking dish. Place half of the fish pieces in one layer across the bottom of the prepared dish. Spread ½ cup of bread crumbs over the fish and pour the beaten eggs over the bread crumbs. Sprinkle with salt, pepper and dillweed. Next, spread the sautéed vegetables over the ingredients in the baking dish and press down lightly.

Sprinkle the feta cheese over the vegetables. Create a second layer with the remaining fish pieces. Season with salt, pepper and a pinch of paprika. Sprinkle another ½ cup of bread crumbs on top. Pour the 3 tablespoons of melted butter over the casserole and top with a dash of lemon juice. Cover the baking dish with aluminum foil. Bake for 30 to 40 minutes or until the fish is opaque.

To serve, remove the baking dish from the oven and cut the casserole into squares.

CRAPPIE ADVICE

The best time to catch crappie is during their feeding time at sunrise or sunset. Crappie live in small- to medium-size lakes and congregate near weeds. One of the benefits of fishing for crappie is that once you find one, there are usually a lot more nearby.

BASIC PAN-FRIED BLUEGILL

Makes: 4 servings   **Prep Time:** 10 to 15 minutes   **Cook Time:** 6 to 10 minutes

INGREDIENTS

- ➤ 1 egg
- ➤ 6 oz. light beer
- ➤ 4 bluegill fillets
- ➤ 1 to 2 C. cracker meal or crushed saltine crackers
- ➤ 2 T. butter or margarine
- ➤ 2 T. vegetable oil
- ➤ 2 lemons
- ➤ 12 cherry tomatoes
- ➤ 4 green onions
- ➤ 1 (3-oz.) jar capers

PREPARATION

In a medium bowl, combine the egg and beer; whisk together until well blended.

Rinse the fillets and pat dry with paper towels. Spread the cracker meal in a shallow pie plate. Dip each bluegill fillet into the egg mixture, letting excess drip off. Next, dredge each fillet in the cracker meal until evenly coated on both sides.

Place the butter and vegetable oil in a large skillet over medium-high heat. Once the butter is melted and the oil is very hot, place the coated fillets in the skillet for 3 to 5 minutes. Turn the fillets over and cook for an additional 3 to 5 minutes or until nicely browned on both sides.

Cut both of the lemons in half. Quarter the cherry tomatoes and chop the green onions. To serve, place one bluegill fillet on each serving plate. Garnish each serving with one lemon half, some cherry tomatoes, some green onions and a few capers.

★★★★ REEL 'EM IN ★★★★

BLUEGILLS FOR THE GREEN FISHERMAN

Bluegills are often the first fish caught by youngsters and novice anglers because they are fairly easy to catch, live in ponds and lakes, eat simple bait like worms and corn kernels and make a good pan fish. If you are not catching bluegills in one area, move around, as bluegills often stay in one place and will not come to you.

BLUEGILL CREAM CHEESE BAKE

Makes: 4 to 6 servings **Prep Time:** 15 minutes **Cook Time:** 20 to 25 minutes

INGREDIENTS

- 1 C. uncooked macaroni pasta
- 1 (3-oz.) pkg. cream cheese, softened
- 1 (10-oz.) can cream of mushroom soup
- ½ small onion
- ½ small green bell pepper
- 2 T. prepared yellow mustard
- ¼ tsp. salt
- ¼ C. milk
- 1½ C. cooked, flaked bluegill
- ½ C. crushed cornflakes

PREPARATION

Preheat the oven to 375°F. Lightly grease a 9"square glass baking dish. Fill a medium pot with lightly salted water. Add the uncooked macaroni and bring the water to a boil. Once the macaroni is tender, after about 8 to 10 minutes, remove the pot from the heat. Drain the pasta and rinse under running water.

In a medium mixing bowl, combine the cream cheese and cream of mushroom soup with an electric mixer. Chop the onion and green pepper. Use a spoon to stir the onion, green pepper and yellow mustard into the cream cheese mixture. Add the salt, milk, bluegill and cooked pasta. Mix everything together until well combined.

Spread the mixture evenly into the prepared baking dish. Sprinkle the cornflakes over top. Bake for 20 to 25 minutes. Cut the casserole into squares and serve.

"There will be days when the fishing is better than one's most optimistic forecast, others when it is far worse. Either is a gain over just staying home."

RODERICK HAIG-BROWN, *Fisherman's Spring*

The two basic types of salmon are:

PACIFIC & ATLANTIC

There are seven species of the Pacific Salmon: Chinook, Sockeye, Coho, Chum, Pink, Masu and Amago. Chinook, Sockeye and Coho are most often sold fresh in markets. Masu and Amago are only found in Asia.

Chinook

Sockeye

Pink Salmon (Spawning Male)

Chinook, or King Salmon, are the largest of the Pacific Salmon. They average between 15 and 40 pounds but can grow as large as 100 pounds. Chinook are a good prize for anglers because of their vibrant orange flesh, buttery texture and high fat content.

Sockeye Salmon, or Red Salmon, are oilier than Chinook, making them ideal for grilling. Sockeye are popular in Japanese sushi and sashimi, and they do not lose their brilliant color when cooked.

An average Coho Salmon, or Silver Salmon, weighs 10 pounds. The flesh is leaner, firmer and more delicate in texture than other salmon and the taste is mild and sweet.

Chum Salmon, or Dog Salmon, have a silvery-blue and green ocean coloration. As the adults are near spawning, they develop purple streaks on their sides. Unlike other salmon, Chum have no spots.

The most numerous salmon are Pink Salmon, or Humpback Salmon. They usually grow from 18" to 24" in length with an average weight of 3 to 5 pounds.

There is only one species of Atlantic Salmon. While Pacific Salmon die shortly after spawning, Atlantic Salmon may live to spawn again. Atlantic Salmon are typically fattier than Pacific Salmon and have bright pink flesh. However, it is very difficult to find wild Atlantic Salmon due to overfishing and pollution. Most Atlantic Salmon are farm-raised and average 10 pounds when harvested.

LEMON GRILLED SALMON

Makes: 6 to 8 servings   **Prep Time:** 15 minutes plus 1 hour marinating   **Cook Time:** 15 to 20 minutes

INGREDIENTS

- ➤ ¾ tsp. dried dillweed
- ➤ ½ tsp. lemon pepper
- ➤ ½ tsp. salt
- ➤ ¼ tsp. garlic powder
- ➤ 1½ to 2 lbs. salmon fillets
- ➤ 2 to 3 green onions
- ➤ ¼ C. brown sugar
- ➤ 3 T. chicken broth
- ➤ 3 T. vegetable oil
- ➤ 3 T. soy sauce
- ➤ 1 small lemon
- ➤ 1 small onion

PREPARATION

In a small bowl, combine the dillweed, lemon pepper, salt and garlic powder; mix well. Sprinkle the seasoning mixture over all sides of the salmon fillets. Place the seasoned fillets in a large resealable plastic bag or shallow glass dish.

Finely chop the green onions. In a medium bowl, combine the green onions, brown sugar, chicken broth, vegetable oil and soy sauce; mix until evenly blended. Pour the brown sugar mixture over the salmon in the bag or dish. Seal the bag or cover the dish with plastic wrap and place in the refrigerator for 1 hour to marinate, turning the fillets over after 30 minutes.

Preheat an outdoor grill to medium heat and lightly oil the grate. Remove the salmon from the refrigerator and discard the marinade. Once the grill is hot, place the salmon, skin side down, on the grill.

Cut the lemon and onion into slices. Place a few lemon and onion slices over each salmon fillet on the grill. Cover the grill and cook for 15 to 20 minutes or until the salmon flakes easily with a fork. Do not turn the salmon over while grilling. Serve immediately.

Grilled salmon is a delicious dish, and grilling is one of the most popular ways to prepare salmon. If you find your fish is coming out overcooked, remember that salmon will keep cooking, even after you've pulled it off the grill. Adjust your cooking time to account for this and see how beautifully your fish turn out.

GARLIC MARINATED BAKED SALMON

Makes: 2 servings   **Prep Time:** 15 minutes plus 1 hour marinating   **Cook Time:** 35 to 45 minutes

INGREDIENTS

- 2 cloves garlic
- 6 T. olive oil
- 1 tsp. dried basil
- 1 tsp. salt
- 1 tsp. pepper
- 1 T. lemon juice
- 1 T. chopped fresh parsley
- 2 (½-lb.) salmon fillets

PREPARATION

Mince the garlic. In a medium glass bowl, combine the garlic, olive oil, basil, salt, pepper, lemon juice and parsley.

Place the salmon fillets, skin side up, in a 9" square glass baking dish. Pour the garlic marinade mixture evenly over the salmon fillets. Cover the baking dish with plastic wrap and place in the refrigerator for 1 hour to marinate, turning the salmon fillets over after 30 minutes.

Preheat the oven to 375°F. Tear off one sheet of aluminum foil large enough to wrap around the salmon fillets. Remove the salmon from the refrigerator. Place the fillets on the aluminum foil. Pour the marinade into a small saucepan over high heat and bring to a boil for 1 minute. Pour the hot marinade over the salmon fillets. Wrap the aluminum foil up and over the salmon, sealing the edges. Place the wrapped fillets in a glass baking dish. Bake for 35 to 45 minutes or until the salmon flakes easily with a fork.

To serve, remove the baking dish from the oven and carefully unwrap the aluminum foil packet. Transfer each fillet to a serving plate and serve immediately.

TACKLE BOX TRIVIA

THE CIRCLE OF LIFE

After a salmon egg hatches, a baby salmonid is born, called an alevin. An alevin looks like a fish with a huge pot belly, which is the remaining egg sac. Next, the salmonid goes through fry stage. A fry is a juvenile salmonid that has absorbed its egg sac and is rearing in the stream. A parr is a large juvenile salmonid, also known as a fingerling. Then, the salmonid grows to a smolt, or a juvenile that has reared in-stream and is preparing to enter the ocean. Smolts exchange their spotted camouflage of the stream for the chrome of the ocean. The grown salmon will return to the stream for spawning.

SALMON & SHRIMP OVER GARLIC RICE

Makes: 4 to 6 servings   **Prep Time:** 20 minutes   **Cook Time:** 25 to 30 minutes

INGREDIENTS

- ½ lb. medium shrimp
- 3 T. butter
- 3 T. flour
- 1½ C. half-and-half
- 1 C. shredded cheddar cheese
- 1 tsp. salt
- ½ tsp. ground mustard
- ¼ tsp. dried dillweed
- Pinch of cayenne pepper
- 4 to 6 (½-lb.) salmon fillets
- ½ C. shredded cheddar cheese
- 3 cloves garlic
- 2 T. butter
- 1 C. uncooked long grain rice
- 2 C. chicken broth

PREPARATION

Preheat the oven to 400°F. Peel and devein the shrimp. Place 3 tablespoons of butter in a large saucepan over medium heat. Once the butter is melted, stir in the flour until smooth. Gradually stir in the half-and-half and mix well. Bring the mixture to a boil for 2 minutes, stirring constantly, or until the sauce is thickened. Stir in the cheddar cheese, salt, ground mustard, dillweed and cayenne pepper. Continue to heat until the cheese is completely melted. Remove the saucepan from the heat and stir in the shrimp.

Rinse the salmon fillets and pat dry with paper towels. Lightly grease a 9 x 13" baking dish. Place the salmon fillets in the baking dish, skin side down. Pour the shrimp and sauce mixture over the salmon and sprinkle with the cheddar cheese. Bake for 25 to 30 minutes or until the salmon flakes easily with a fork.

Meanwhile, mince the garlic. Place the remaining 2 tablespoons of butter in a medium saucepan over medium-high heat. Once the butter is melted, stir in the garlic and sauté until tender and fragrant. Add the rice and sauté, stirring often, for 2 minutes. Add the chicken broth and bring the mixture to a boil. Reduce the heat to medium-low, cover and cook for 15 minutes or until the rice is tender.

To serve, place a bed of hot cooked rice on each serving plate. Remove the baking dish from the oven and place a serving of salmon and shrimp with sauce over the rice.

"Scholars have long known that fishing eventually turns men into philosophers. Unfortunately, it is almost impossible to buy decent tackle on a philosopher's salary."

PATRICK F. MCMANUS

ORIENTAL SALMON STEAKS

Makes: 4 servings   **Prep Time:** 15 minutes plus 1 hour marinating   **Cook Time:** 6 to 10 minutes

INGREDIENTS

- 1 to 2 green onions
- 1 clove garlic
- 1 (½") piece gingerroot
- ⅓ C. soy sauce
- ¼ C. orange juice concentrate
- 2 T. vegetable oil
- 2 T. tomato sauce
- 1 tsp. lemon juice
- ½ tsp. prepared yellow mustard
- 4 (½-lb.) salmon steaks, about 1" thick
- 1 T. olive oil

PREPARATION

Chop the green onions and mince the garlic. Mince or finely grate the gingerroot. In a small bowl, combine the green onions, garlic, gingerroot, soy sauce, orange juice concentrate, vegetable oil, tomato sauce, lemon juice and mustard. Mix everything together until well combined.

Place the salmon steaks in an even layer in a 9 x 13" glass baking dish. Pour the marinade mixture over the salmon, turning to coat both sides. Cover the baking dish with plastic wrap and place in the refrigerator for 1 hour to marinate, turning the steaks over after 30 minutes.

Preheat an outdoor grill to high heat and lightly oil the grate. Remove the baking dish from the refrigerator. Pour the marinade into a small saucepan. Place the saucepan over high heat and bring the marinade to a boil for 1 minute.

Using a pastry brush, brush the salmon steaks lightly with olive oil. Grill the steaks for 3 to 5 minutes on one side. Gently turn the steaks over and grill for an additional 3 to 5 minutes. Brush the marinade over the salmon as it is grilling. The salmon is done when it flakes easily with a fork. Discard any remaining marinade. Transfer the grilled salmon to a serving dish and serve immediately.

★★★★ REEL 'EM IN ★★★★

THE SEARCH FOR SALMON

Adult salmon go where they must to find food and a comfortable water temperature. Their search for 53° to 57°F water may take them miles from shore or within casting distance of piers. This makes it difficult to catch salmon consistently. But, as spawning time nears, salmon will gather near tributary streams where finding and catching them becomes easier.

ALASKAN SALMON CHOWDER

Makes: 4 to 6 servings **Prep Time:** 10 minutes **Cook Time:** 30 minutes

INGREDIENTS

- 1 small onion
- 2 to 3 stalks celery
- ½ small green bell pepper
- 1 clove garlic
- 1 (14½-oz.) can chicken broth, divided
- 2 to 3 potatoes
- 2 large carrots
- 1 tsp. seasoned salt
- ½ tsp. dried dillweed
- 1 small zucchini
- 1 (14¾-oz.) can cream-style corn
- 1 (12-oz.) can evaporated milk
- 2 C. cooked, flaked salmon

PREPARATION

Chop the onion, celery and green pepper. Mince the garlic. In a large saucepan or pot over medium-high heat, place the onion, celery, green pepper and garlic. Add about ¼ cup of the chicken broth to the saucepan and cook until the vegetables are tender.

Meanwhile, clean, peel and dice the potatoes. Slice the carrots. Once the onions are tender, stir in the potatoes, carrots, seasoned salt, dillweed and remaining chicken broth. Cover the saucepan and let the mixture simmer for 20 minutes or until all the vegetables are tender.

Thinly slice the zucchini and add to the saucepan. Simmer for an additional 5 minutes. Slowly stir in the cream-style corn, evaporated milk and salmon. Cook for 1 to 2 additional minutes or until all ingredients are heated through.

To serve, ladle the salmon chowder into bowls and serve with oyster crackers or slices of crusty bread on the side.

"The charm of fishing is that it is the pursuit of what is elusive but attainable— a perpetual series of occasions for hope."

— JOHN BUCHAN

SALMON FILLETS IN CREAMY DILL SAUCE

Makes: 4 servings **Prep Time:** 5 to 10 minutes **Cook Time:** 30 to 40 minutes

INGREDIENTS

- 1½ C. mayonnaise
- ½ C. prepared yellow mustard
- 1 tsp. chopped fresh thyme
- 1 tsp. dried oregano
- 1 tsp. chopped fresh basil
- 4 (½-lb.) salmon fillets
- 2 tsp. dried dillweed

PREPARATION

Preheat the oven to 375°F. In a medium bowl, combine the mayonnaise and mustard. Stir in the thyme, oregano and basil; mix well. Set aside and refrigerate half of the mayonnaise mixture until ready to serve.

Place the salmon fillets, skin side down, on a lightly greased baking sheet. Spread a generous amount of the remaining mayonnaise mixture over the fillets. Sprinkle the dillweed over the fillets. Bake for 30 to 40 minutes or until the salmon flakes easily with a fork.

To serve, transfer the baked salmon fillets to a serving dish and serve with the reserved mayonnaise mixture on the side.

"This planet is covered with sordid men who demand that he who spends time fishing shall show returns in fish."

— LEONIDAS HUBBARD, JR.

★★★★ FISH TALES ★★★★

THE SIZE OF SALMON

The size of a salmon is usually directly related to its age. Pink Salmon are the smallest and have the shortest lifespan, usually two years. But Chinook Salmon can live up to nine years and some can grow to more than 100 pounds.

THE FINE ART OF COOLER PACKING

Whether you are planning a daylong fishing trip or a weeklong hunting/camping trip, at the very least you will want some snacks, and more likely, you'll want some full-blown meals. Here are some tricks you can use to pack your cooler for full satisfaction.

SEPARATE YOUR STASH. Sometimes, two is better than one. Two coolers can allow you to separate food items like drinks and food or perishables and non-perishables, allowing you to pack the two different groups two different ways. When packing in multiple coolers, use coolers in different colors so you can tell them apart, or label them with masking tape and a marker.

SURROUND YOUR DRINKS. To keep drinks extra-cold, pack your cooler with a layer of ice on the bottom, add your drinks, and then pack ice between and over top of them.

BLOCKS VS. CUBES. If you are going on a long trip, consider using a block of ice instead of ice cubes. Ice blocks melt more slowly than ice cubes, keeping your food fresh and cool longer.

AVOID SOGGINESS. Ice is great for items that you don't mind getting wet as the ice melts, like cans of soda. Sometimes, however, melting ice can make your food soggy. To avoid this, consider using ice packs sealed in plastic bags.

KEEP TRACK OF PERISHABLES AND BREAKABLES. During your trip, it's important to make sure your perishables don't, well, perish, before you've had the chance to use them. Make sure you know where they are in your cooler, and that they are positioned to stay cool at all times. Similarly, make sure you know where any glass or other breakable items are, and be careful moving coolers with these items in them.

A Great **TROPHY FISH**

Fish in the pike family have long, skinny bodies and duck bill-shaped snouts. Three of the most popular fish in the pike family are the Northern Pike, Muskellunge and Pickerel. Both are often displayed as trophy fish.

Northern Pike live in the Great Lakes, the upper Mississippi Valley of North America and in smaller lakes in Canada, as well as in the northern waters of Europe and Asia. They usually weigh between 2 and 10 pounds but can weigh more than 40 pounds and grow to a length of 4 feet.

Muskellunge, or Musky, are the largest fish in the pike family. The lifespan of Muskellunge is about 25 years and they live in the quiet lakes and rivers of southern Canada. Muskellunge can also be found in the Great Lakes, the upper Mississippi Valley, the St. Lawrence River and the Ohio River. Most Muskellunge are between 3 and 4 feet long and weigh anywhere from 5 to 36 pounds. Many anglers consider Muskellunge to be one of the best fish to eat.

Pickerel is the smaller member of the pike family. The three subspecies of pickerel are: Redfin, Grass and Chain. Redfin and Chain Pickerel live in the waters from Maine to Florida, while the Grass Pickerel are usually found in the Mississippi Valley. Pickerel are known for their stubborn fighting ability, large mouths and greedy appetites.

Northern Pike

Musky

Pickerel

TACKLE BOX

This table shows the most preferred gear for catching Pike and Musky.

GEAR	DESCRIPTION
Rod	Medium to Heavy Medium
Line	10–17 pound test with a black steel 30-pound leader
Lure	Crank baits, spinner baits, top water lures
Lure Color	Red, chartreuse, brown, red and white, black and white

GRILLED PIKE WITH CUCUMBERS

Makes: 6 to 8 servings   **Prep Time:** 20 to 25 minutes   **Cook Time:** 12 to 16 minutes

INGREDIENTS

- ➤ 1 tsp. vegetable oil
- ➤ 6 T. pine nuts
- ➤ 1 cucumber
- ➤ 2 T. butter or margarine
- ➤ 6 green onions
- ➤ 1 (2- to 3-lb.) pike fillet
- ➤ 1 tsp. salt
- ➤ 1 to 2 tsp. pepper
- ➤ 1 lemon

PREPARATION

Preheat an outdoor grill to medium-high heat and lightly oil the grate. To brown the pine nuts, heat the vegetable oil in a medium skillet over medium-low heat. When the oil is hot, stir in the pine nuts. Sauté for 1 minute or until the pine nuts are golden brown, stirring constantly. Transfer the pine nuts to paper towels to drain; set aside.

Peel, seed and thinly slice the cucumber. Melt the butter in the same skillet over low heat. Once the butter is melted, add the cucumber; sauté for 10 to 15 minutes or until the cucumbers are translucent. Slice the green onions diagonally. Add the green onions to the skillet and sauté for an additional 2 minutes. Remove the skillet from the heat and stir in the pine nuts. Cover the skillet to keep warm.

When the grill is hot, place the pike fillet on the lightly-oiled grate. Grill for 6 to 8 minutes per side or until the fish flakes easily with a fork. Remove the grilled fish to a serving dish and season with salt and pepper.

To serve, cut the pike fillet into four serving-size pieces. Cut the lemon into six wedges. Squeeze two of the wedges over the fish. Ladle the cucumber sauce over the fish and garnish the servings with the remaining four lemon wedges.

★★★★ FISH TALES ★★★★

GROWING PAINS

Similar to counting the rings in a tree trunk, scientists count the rings in the fish's otolith to determine its age. The otolith is a bone located just behind the ear and is used for hearing. One ring equals one year. In addition, scales can sometimes be used to determine a fish's lifespan. The scales have lines that are similar to the lines on the otolith. Again, one line equals one year.

PARMESAN BAKED PIKE IN TOMATO SAUCE

Makes: 4 servings **Prep Time:** 10 minutes **Cook Time:** 12 to 15 minutes

INGREDIENTS

- 1 (1½-lb.) pike fillet
- ⅓ C. olive oil
- 2 T. lemon juice
- ½ C. fine dry bread crumbs
- ½ C. grated Parmesan cheese
- 1 T. chopped fresh parsley
- Pinch of salt
- Pinch of pepper
- 1 medium tomato
- 1 T. chopped or whole capers
- 1 T. chopped fresh basil
- 2 T. dry white wine
- 1 T. butter
- Salt and pepper
- Grated Parmesan cheese

PREPARATION

Preheat the oven to 500°F. Lightly grease a baking sheet. Cut the fillet into four serving-size pieces.

Combine the olive oil and lemon juice in a medium bowl. In a shallow pie plate, combine the bread crumbs, Parmesan cheese, parsley, salt and pepper; mix well. Dip the fillets into the olive oil mixture and then into the bread crumb mixture, turning to coat both sides. Place the coated fish pieces on the prepared baking sheet. Bake for 12 to 15 minutes.

Meanwhile, chop the tomato. Place the tomato in a medium saucepan over medium-high heat. Add the capers and basil. Sauté for 1 to 2 minutes and slowly pour in the white wine. Bring the mixture to a boil and add the butter in small pieces, stirring just until the butter melts. Remove the saucepan from the heat and season the sauce with salt and pepper to taste.

To serve, transfer each baked fish piece to a serving plate. Drizzle a generous amount of the tomato sauce mixture over each serving. Top each serving with a sprinkling of additional Parmesan cheese.

FISH & TIPS

1. Clean the fish properly before storing.

2. If storing fish in the refrigerator, make sure the temperature is below 40°F.

3. Do not let cooked fish sit at room temperature for more than 2 hours.

4. Wrap individual pieces of fish in plastic wrap or foil and then place in a freezer bag, allowing you to take out only the number of pieces that need to be prepared.

5. Freeze fresh fish as soon as possible; never re-freeze fish that has been previously frozen and thawed.

6. Thaw frozen fish in the refrigerator or in cold water, changing the water every 30 minutes. Never thaw fish at room temperature.

PIKE FINGERS IN RAGOUT SAUCE

Makes: 6 to 8 servings **Prep Time:** 25 minutes **Cook Time:** 10 minutes

INGREDIENTS

- 6 fresh artichoke bottoms*
- 1 (3-lb.) pike fillet
- 1 C. flour
- 1 tsp. salt
- ½ tsp. pepper
- 1 T. butter or margarine
- 1 T. olive oil
- 3 tomatoes
- 1 tsp. butter or margarine
- 1 tsp. olive oil
- ½ C. finely chopped mushrooms
- 2 T. finely chopped black olives
- ⅓ C. Chardonnay wine
- 3 T. chopped fresh parsley
- 1 T. lemon juice

PREPARATION

Place the artichoke bottoms in a large pot of lightly salted water. Place the pot over medium-high heat and bring the water to a boil. Continue to cook until the artichoke bottoms are tender, about 10 minutes. Remove the artichoke bottoms from the saucepan and let cool slightly before dicing.

Remove any skin from the fillet and cut the fish into strips that are 3" to 4" in length. In a small bowl, combine the flour, salt and pepper; mix well. Dust each strip with the seasoned flour on all sides.

Place 1 tablespoon of butter and 1 tablespoon of olive oil in a large skillet over medium-high heat. Once the butter is melted and the oil is hot, place the coated pike strips in the skillet and cook until golden brown, turning to cook both sides. Remove the pike from the skillet and keep warm.

Dice and seed the tomatoes and set aside. Place the diced artichoke bottoms into the same skillet over medium heat. Add the additional 1 teaspoon of butter and 1 teaspoon of olive oil. Stir in the mushrooms, black olives, Chardonnay, parsley and lemon juice. Mix in the tomatoes. Continue to cook until heated through. Add the pike strips to the skillet and turn until coated in sauce. Remove the pike strips to a serving dish and spoon the remaining sauce over top.

* An artichoke bottom is the fleshy base section of an artichoke. Artichoke bottoms have a tender texture and flavorful taste, similar to the artichoke heart.

"Fishing is a discipline in the equality of men, for all men are equal before fish."

— HERBERT HOOVER

CHEESE-STUFFED PIKE CORN CAKES

Makes: 6 to 8 servings **Prep Time:** 20 minutes **Cook Time:** 10 to 15 minutes

INGREDIENTS

- 1½ C. biscuit baking mix
- 1 egg
- 1⅓ C. milk
- 2 C. fresh or frozen sweet corn
- ½ C. seasoned cornmeal breading mix
- 1 (8-oz.) pkg. cream cheese, softened
- ½ tsp. Cajun seasoning
- 1 C. finely shredded sharp cheddar cheese
- 1 tsp. dried basil
- 1 (2- to 2½-lb.) pike fillet
- 1 to 2 T. vegetable oil

PREPARATION

In a blender or food processor, combine the biscuit baking mix, egg, milk, corn and cornmeal breading mix. Process on high until the ingredients are well combined but the corn is still lumpy. Transfer the batter to a medium bowl.

In a separate bowl, combine the cream cheese, Cajun seasoning, cheddar cheese and basil; mix until well combined.

Cut the pike fillet into serving-size pieces that are about ¾" thick. Use a sharp thin knife to split each piece in half again, being careful not to cut all the way through. Fold each fish piece open like a book. Place a few spoonfuls of the cream cheese mixture on one side of each fillet and fold the fish back over the filling.

Place a large deep skillet over medium-high heat. Add the vegetable oil to the skillet. Once the oil is hot, place a generous spoonful of the batter in the pan. Set one of the cheese-stuffed fish pieces over the batter and spoon more batter over the fish. Heat until the batter begins to brown. Gently and quickly turn the fish over to the other side and heat until the batter is golden brown. Cut a small slit in one side of the coating to make sure the fish is opaque and cooked through. Repeat with the remaining batter and fish pieces.

★★★★ FISH TALES ★★★★

WHAT'S IN A NAME?

Walleyed-Pike is neither a walleye nor a pike; it is a member of the perch family. These fish are found mainly in freshwater lakes of the northern United States and adjoining areas of Canada.

BREADED BAKED PIKE

Makes: 6 servings   **Prep Time:** 10 minutes plus 30 minutes soaking   **Cook Time:** 25 minutes

INGREDIENTS

- 1 (2-lb.) pike fillet
- 1 C. milk
- ½ C. dry bread crumbs
- ½ tsp. salt
- ½ tsp. pepper
- 1 T. chopped fresh parsley
- 1 green onion
- ½ C. butter or margarine, melted
- 1 lemon

PREPARATION

Cut the pike fillet into four to six serving-size pieces. Place the fish pieces in a medium bowl and pour the milk over top. Cover the bowl and place in the refrigerator for 30 minutes to soak.

Preheat the oven to 350°F. Grease a 9 x 13" glass baking dish; set aside. In a shallow pie plate, combine the bread crumbs, salt, pepper and parsley. Remove the pike from the refrigerator and discard the milk. Roll the fish pieces in the bread crumb mixture until evenly coated. Place the coated fish pieces in the prepared baking dish.

Chop the green onion and sprinkle over the fish in the baking dish. Drizzle the melted butter over the fish. Bake, uncovered, for 25 minutes or until the fish flakes easily with a fork. To serve, cut the lemon into wedges. Place one fish piece on each serving plate and garnish with a wedge of lemon.

This splendid pike is an armful. Minnesota guide Jeff Sundin recommends using smaller pike (about 24 inches in length) for most recipes and releasing the larger examples—as pictured here—to fight another day. Remember that when frozen, Northern Pike don't keep as well some other popular fish species.

A TALE of TWO FISH

Walleye is a freshwater fish that is native to Canada and the northern United States.

Walleyes have been raised in hatcheries for more than a century and have been released in lakes and rivers to restock the population or place more walleye on top of existing populations. Walleyes can show a considerable amount of variation from one body of water to another.

Because of its great taste, Walleye are an often sought-after fish and the top prize for many anglers.

Sauger is a fish very similar to the Walleye. However, Saugers are usually smaller than Walleyes and can be distinguished by their spotted dorsal fin, lack of a white splotch on the anal fin and by their more brassy color. Saugers are more common in rivers while Walleyes are more typically found in lakes and reservoirs. Like Walleyes, Saugers are a good catch for any fisherman.

Walleye and Sauger do sometimes mate and their offspring are called Saugeye. These fish can exhibit traits from both species, but generally carry the dark blotches that are characteristic of the Sauger.

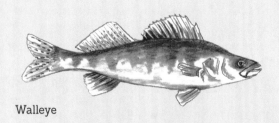

Walleye

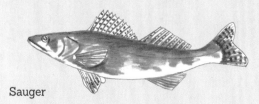

Sauger

"I always try to let the walleye tell me what it wants."

GARY ROACH

GRILLED WALLEYE WITH FRUIT CHUTNEY

Makes: 4 to 6 servings   **Prep Time:** 15 minutes plus 15 minutes marinating   **Cook Time:** 15 minutes

INGREDIENTS

- 4 to 6 (½-lb.) walleye fillets
- 2 cloves garlic
- 2 T. olive oil
- Salt and pepper
- 1 red apple
- 1 orange
- 1 medium onion
- 1 clove garlic
- 1 C. diced cantaloupe
- ½ C. vinegar
- 1 C. dry white wine
- 2 T. olive oil
- 1 T. dried oregano
- Salt and pepper

PREPARATION

Place the walleye fillets in a large bowl. Mince two cloves of garlic. Sprinkle the garlic and olive oil over the fillets. Cover the bowl with plastic wrap and place in the refrigerator for 15 minutes to marinate.

Preheat an outdoor grill to medium-high heat and lightly oil the grate. Tear one piece of aluminum foil large enough to wrap around all of the fish fillets. Remove the fillets from the refrigerator and discard any remaining garlic or oil from the bowl. Sprinkle the fish with salt and pepper. Place the fish on the aluminum foil and wrap the foil up and over the fish, pinching the sides to enclose the fish. Place the wrapped packet on the grill over indirect heat. Grill for about 15 minutes or until the fish flakes easily with a fork.

Meanwhile, prepare the fruit chutney. Dice the apple, orange and onion. Mince the remaining garlic clove. In a medium bowl, combine the apple, orange, onion, garlic, cantaloupe, vinegar, white wine, olive oil and oregano. Season with salt and pepper to taste and mix well.

To serve, remove the fish from the grill and carefully unwrap the packet. Transfer each grilled fillet to a serving dish. Garnish each serving with a generous amount of the fruit chutney.

★★★★ TACKLE BOX TRIVIA ★★★★

THE PRICE OF GLORY

Each year, an average of 30 million anglers spend about $40 billion on fishing equipment and fishing-related expenditures, including licenses and fees, as well as food, lodging and transportation during fishing trips. That is an average of more than $1,000 per fisherman per year.

THE NATIONAL SURVEY OF HUNTING, FISHING, AND WILDLIFE-ASSOCIATED RECREATION

COOKING FISH & GAME

BARBECUED WALLEYE SKEWERS

Makes: 6 to 8 servings **Prep Time:** 15 minutes plus 8 hours marinating **Cook Time:** 5 to 10 minutes

INGREDIENTS

- ➤ 1½ to 2 lbs. walleye pieces
- ➤ 1 sweet red pepper
- ➤ 1 green bell pepper
- ➤ 1 yellow bell pepper
- ➤ 1 large onion
- ➤ 2 T. soy sauce
- ➤ 2 T. teriyaki sauce
- ➤ 1 T. honey
- ➤ 1 T. hoisin sauce
- ➤ 1 T. Cajun seasoning
- ➤ ½ tsp. Worcestershire sauce
- ➤ Pinch of salt
- ➤ Pinch of pepper
- ➤ Wooden skewers

PREPARATION

Cut the walleye into large bite-size cubes or pieces. Cut the red, green and yellow peppers into 1" squares. Chop the onion into 1" pieces. Place the fish, peppers and onions in a large bowl.

In a medium bowl, combine the soy sauce, teriyaki sauce, honey, hoisin sauce, Cajun seasoning, Worcestershire sauce, salt and pepper. Mix well and pour the marinade over the fish and vegetables in the bowl. Cover the bowl with plastic wrap and place in the refrigerator for 8 hours or overnight. Soak the wooden skewers in a bowl of water for at least 1 hour prior to grilling.

Preheat the grill to medium-high heat and lightly oil the grate. Remove the bowl from the refrigerator and discard the marinade. Thread the fish pieces, peppers and onions onto the skewers, pressing the pieces against each other. The fish pieces will reduce in size during grilling so be sure to surround them snugly with vegetables.

Place the skewers on the grill and cook for 5 to 10 minutes or until the fish pieces turn opaque and the vegetables are tender; turn to cook all sides. If desired, brush the fish and vegetables with additional soy sauce or teriyaki sauce during grilling.

★★★★ TACKLE BOX TRIVIA ★★★★

TROPHY CASE

Because of their thick white fillets, walleyes are one of the most sought-after freshwater fish. The average caught walleye weighs in at just over 1 pound and is 14" in length. The official world-record walleye was caught in 1982 and weighed 22 pounds, 11 ounces. However, an unofficial world record has been held since 1960 for a 25-pound walleye.

FISH TACOS

Makes: 6 servings **Prep Time:** 15 minutes plus 8 hours marinating **Cook Time:** 15 minutes

INGREDIENTS

- ¾ C. flour
- ½ tsp. baking powder
- ½ tsp. dried oregano
- ½ tsp. garlic powder
- ½ tsp. chili powder
- ¼ tsp. cayenne pepper
- Pinch of salt
- Pinch of pepper
- 1 egg yolk
- 4 to 6 oz. beer
- Oil for frying
- ½ C. mayonnaise
- 1 T. chopped fresh cilantro
- Juice of ½ lime
- 1 ripe avocado
- 1 to 1½ lbs. walleye pieces
- 6 (6") flour tortillas
- 1 lime
- 2 C. shredded lettuce

PREPARATION

In a medium bowl, combine the flour, baking powder, oregano, garlic powder, chili powder, cayenne pepper, salt, pepper, egg yolk and beer. Mix until well combined. Cover the bowl with plastic wrap and place in the refrigerator for 8 hours or overnight.

In a large deep skillet, place 2" of oil. Heat the oil to 375°F. In a small bowl, combine the mayonnaise, cilantro and lime juice. Cut the avocado into slices and chop the walleye into bite-size pieces. Remove the batter from the refrigerator.

Drop the walleye pieces into the batter until well-coated. When the oil is hot, place one or two pieces at a time into the skillet and fry for 3 to 5 minutes, turning the pieces after 2 minutes. Remove the fried walleye pieces to paper towels to drain and repeat with the remaining fish and batter.

Meanwhile, wrap the flour tortillas in damp paper towels. Microwave the wrapped tortillas for 1 minute or until they are soft and pliable. Cut the lime into wedges.

To assemble a taco, place a few pieces of fried fish in a tortilla. Top with a few slices of avocado, a little shredded lettuce and a drizzling of the mayonnaise sauce. Repeat with remaining ingredients. Squeeze a little fresh lime juice over each taco before folding and serving.

★★★★ FISH TALES ★★★★

IN THE EYE OF THE BEHOLDER

Walleyes can be identified by well-defined sharp canine teeth on their jaws and the roof of their mouths. They also have oversized pearlescent eyes that allow them to see in murky water and during the night. It is these opaque eyes that give walleyes their name. Walleyes are generally yellow to olive brown on their backs and sides, with white bellies.

WALLEYE & KRAUT SANDWICHES

Makes: 4 servings   **Prep Time:** 15 minutes   **Cook Time:** 12 to 16 minutes

INGREDIENTS

- 1½ C. cooked, flaked walleye
- ½ C. sauerkraut, drained
- ¼ C. chopped dill pickles
- ¼ C. mayonnaise
- 1 T. horseradish sauce
- ¼ C. butter or margarine, softened
- 8 slices rye bread
- 4 slices Swiss cheese
- 2 T. butter or margarine

PREPARATION

In a medium bowl, combine the walleye, sauerkraut, dill pickles, mayonnaise and horseradish sauce; mix until well combined.

Use the ¼ cup of butter to spread over one side of each rye bread slice. Divide and spread the walleye mixture evenly onto the unbuttered side of four slices of bread. Top with the slices of Swiss cheese. Place the remaining four bread slices on top, buttered side out.

Melt the remaining 2 tablespoons of butter in a medium skillet over medium heat. Once the butter is melted, place the sandwiches in the skillet and grill for 3 to 4 minutes on each side or until the bread is golden brown and the filling is heated through.

To serve, place each sandwich on a plate and cut diagonally into halves. Serve with chips on the side.

"It has always been my private conviction that any man who pits his intelligence against a fish and loses has it coming."

JOHN STEINBECK

HORSERADISH WALLEYE

Makes: 6 servings **Prep Time:** 10 minutes plus 30 minutes marinating **Cook Time:** 10 minutes

INGREDIENTS

- ➢ 6 (½-lb.) walleye fillets
- ➢ 1 (12-oz.) bottle herb & garlic marinade
- ➢ 1 tsp. seasoned salt
- ➢ 1 tsp. lemon pepper
- ➢ ¼ C. butter or margarine
- ➢ 2 T. horseradish sauce
- ➢ 1 tsp. dried dillweed

PREPARATION

Place the walleye fillets in a resealable plastic bag. Pour desired amount of the marinade over the fish and seal the bag. Place the bag flat in the refrigerator for 30 minutes to marinate. Turn the bag over after 15 minutes.

After 30 minutes, remove the walleye fillets from the refrigerator and discard the marinade. Sprinkle the seasoned salt and lemon pepper over the fillets.

Preheat an outdoor grill or oven broiler to high heat. Place the seasoned walleye fillets on the lightly-oiled grill and cook for 5 minutes on each side, or until the fish flakes easily with a fork. If using a broiler, place the fish 6" under the heat and cook for 3 to 5 minutes per side. Remove the fish to a serving dish and keep warm.

Place the butter in a small saucepan over medium heat. When the butter is melted, remove the saucepan from the heat. Stir in the horseradish sauce. Spoon the butter sauce over the fish and sprinkle with the dillweed. Serve immediately.

Walleye, especially those in lakes, begin spawning in the late winter and early spring. This means they begin traveling up the lake's tributaries. If fishing for walleye during this time, try staking a spot along one of the tributaries rather than on the lake itself.

FISH & SHELLFISH

Seafood is a rich source of protein, vitamins and minerals. The American Heart Association recommends eating seafood at least twice a week as part of a heart-healthy lifestyle. The USDA recommends that Americans should eat more fish, especially fish containing heart-healthy Omega-3 fatty acids.

Some of the most popular types of seafood include shrimp, crab, halibut, tilapia and haddock. Trout and salmon are often considered sea fish rather than freshwater fish since they spend a majority of their lives in salt water. However, most trout and salmon return to fresh water to spawn.

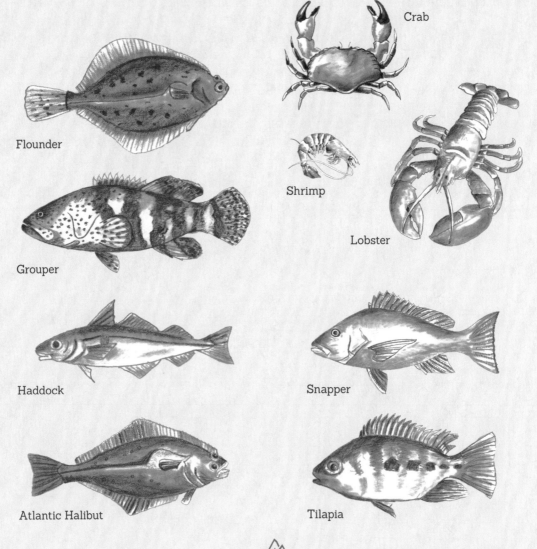

Crab

Flounder

Shrimp

Lobster

Grouper

Haddock

Snapper

Atlantic Halibut

Tilapia

Crab is a white or yellowish-white meat with a sweet, delicate taste. It comes in flakes or tender clumps and is best when boiled or steamed.

Flounder is a white meat with mild flavor, fine texture and small flake. It is best when grilled in a basket, broiled, baked, fried or sautéed.

Grouper is a white meat with a moderate flavor, firm texture and large flake. It is best when grilled, broiled, baked, fried or sautéed

Haddock is a white meat with a sweet, delicate taste, moderate to firm texture and fine flake. It is best when grilled in a basket, baked, fried or sautéed.

Halibut is a white meat with a mild and slightly sweet flavor and a fine, firm texture. It is best when grilled, steamed, sautéed, baked or broiled with the skin on.

Lobster has a delicate flavor and tender texture. It is best when boiled, steamed or broiled.

Shrimp is firm and delicately flavored. It is usually gray, brown or bluish when raw, then pink and white when cooked. It is best when grilled, broiled, poached, baked, sautéed, fried or steamed.

Snapper is a white meat with a mild, delicate flavor and moderately firm texture. It is best when grilled, broiled, baked, sautéed or steamed.

Tilapia has white or pinkish flesh with a sweet, mild taste and firm texture. It is best when grilled, broiled, baked, fried or steamed.

This is a whale of a fish, but is it a fish tale? You decide! Either way, if you want to catch one just as big, keep an eye out for seagulls. If seagulls have gathered to feed on small fish, it's likely the large fish you want to catch will be right behind.

SHRIMP OR SCALLOP CILANTRO LIME SALAD

Makes: 4 to 6 servings **Prep Time:** 15 to 20 minutes plus 1 hour marinating **Cook Time:** 6 to 10 minutes

INGREDIENTS

- ➤ 1 C. orange juice
- ➤ 3 T. chopped fresh basil
- ➤ 18 sea scallops or 30 medium shrimp, peeled and deveined
- ➤ Wooden skewers
- ➤ 1 clove garlic
- ➤ 1 green onion
- ➤ ¼ C. sugar
- ➤ ¼ C. olive oil
- ➤ 2 T. lime juice
- ➤ 2 T. rice wine vinegar
- ➤ 1½ tsp. minced fresh cilantro
- ➤ 2 cucumbers
- ➤ 1 head bibb lettuce
- ➤ 4 C. mixed baby lettuce
- ➤ 30 yellow pear-shaped tomatoes
- ➤ 30 red pear-shaped tomatoes

PREPARATION

In a medium bowl, combine the orange juice and basil. Add the scallops or shrimp, tossing until evenly coated. Cover the bowl with plastic wrap and place in the refrigerator for 1 hour to marinate. Soak the wooden skewers in a bowl of water for at least 1 hour as well.

Meanwhile, prepare the vinaigrette. Mince the garlic and chop the green onion. In a jar with a tight-fitting lid, combine the garlic, green onion, sugar, olive oil, lime juice, vinegar and cilantro. Close the jar and shake vigorously until the dressing is well combined.

Preheat an outdoor grill to medium heat and lightly oil the grate. Remove the scallops or shrimp from the refrigerator and discard the marinade. Thread the scallops or shrimp onto the skewers and grill for 3 to 5 minutes on each side. Remove from the grill and slide the scallops or shrimp onto a plate and keep warm.

Cut the cucumbers into thin slices and tear the bibb lettuce into pieces. In a salad bowl, toss together the bibb lettuce and mixed baby lettuce. Add the cucumbers, tomatoes and grilled scallops or shrimp. Top with the vinaigrette and toss together until well combined.

★★★★ FISH TALES ★★★★

SO SHRIMPLE

Because of their physical similarities, many people are confused about the difference between shrimp and prawns. Both have long slender bodies with lots of legs, a head at the front and long antennae. However, prawns have abdominal side plates that overlap like tiles from front to tail. But shrimp have a center segment that overlaps the plates in front and behind. As far as taste goes, there is no discernible difference. For best flavor, always try to purchase fresh prawns or shrimp rather than ones that have been pre-cooked and frozen.

HALIBUT IN ORANGE SAUCE

Makes: 4 to 6 servings **Prep Time:** 15 minutes plus 30 minutes marinating **Cook Time:** 10 to 20 minutes

INGREDIENTS

- ➤ 4 to 6 halibut steaks
- ➤ 2 green onions
- ➤ ½ C. orange juice
- ➤ 1 T. lime or lemon juice
- ➤ 1 T. vegetable oil
- ➤ ¼ tsp. ground ginger
- ➤ ⅛ tsp. salt
- ➤ ½ C. flour
- ➤ ¼ tsp. salt
- ➤ ⅛ tsp. pepper
- ➤ 2 T. vegetable oil
- ➤ 1 orange

PREPARATION

Place the halibut steaks in a 9 x 13" glass baking dish. Slice the green onions diagonally. In a small bowl, combine the green onions, orange juice, lime juice, 1 tablespoon of vegetable oil, ground ginger and salt; mix well. Pour the orange juice mixture over the halibut. Cover and place the baking dish in the refrigerator for 30 minutes to marinate.

Meanwhile, in a shallow pie plate, combine the flour, salt and pepper; mix until blended. After 30 minutes, remove the halibut from the refrigerator and pour the marinade into a separate bowl. Dip the halibut steaks in the seasoned flour, turning to coat both sides.

Heat the remaining 2 tablespoons of vegetable oil in a large skillet over medium-high heat. Once the oil is hot, cook the steaks for 10 minutes per inch of thickness, measured at the thickest part of the steaks. Turn the steaks halfway through cooking time. The fish is done when it flakes easily with a fork. Remove the halibut to a serving plate and keep warm.

Pour the reserved marinade into the same skillet over medium-high heat. Cook, stirring often, until the sauce is reduced to about ⅓ cup. Pour the sauce over the halibut. Cut the orange into round slices and place around the halibut on the serving dish.

"Many men go fishing all of their lives without knowing that it is not fish they are after."

— HENRY DAVID THOREAU

HOT & SPICY GROUPER OR SNAPPER

Makes: 4 servings **Prep Time:** 15 to 20 minutes plus 1 hour marinating **Cook Time:** 10 minutes

INGREDIENTS

- ➤ 4 (½-lb.) grouper or snapper fillets
- ➤ ¼ C. lemon juice
- ➤ 2 T. hot pepper sauce
- ➤ 1 T. vegetable oil
- ➤ 2 tsp. grated fresh gingerroot
- ➤ ½ tsp. salt
- ➤ ¼ tsp. pepper
- ➤ 1 T. sesame seeds
- ➤ 1 T. minced fresh parsley

PREPARATION

Place the grouper or snapper fillets in a 9 x 13" glass baking dish. In a small bowl, combine the lemon juice, hot pepper sauce, vegetable oil, gingerroot, salt, pepper and 2 tablespoons of water; mix well. Divide the liquid mixture in half. Place half in the refrigerator and pour the remaining half over the grouper or snapper. Cover and place the baking dish in the refrigerator for 1 hour to marinate, turning the fillets after 30 minutes.

Meanwhile, toast the sesame seeds. Preheat the oven to 350°F. Arrange the sesame seeds in an even layer on a baking sheet and bake for 8 minutes or until the seeds are lightly browned.

Preheat an outdoor grill to medium-high heat and lightly oil the grate. Remove the fish from the refrigerator and discard the marinade. Grill the fish for 5 minutes on each side, basting often with the reserved marinade.

To serve, transfer the grilled fish to a serving dish. Sprinkle the toasted sesame seeds over top and garnish with the parsley.

"If people concentrated on the really important things in life, there'd be a shortage of fishing poles."

— DOUG LARSON

ALMOND-TOPPED COD OR HADDOCK

Makes: 4 servings **Prep Time:** 10 to 15 minutes **Cook Time:** 18 to 20 minutes

INGREDIENTS

- ➤ 1 T. butter or margarine
- ➤ 1 small onion
- ➤ 4 (½-lb.) cod or haddock fillets
- ➤ 1 tsp. seasoned salt
- ➤ ½ tsp. dried dillweed
- ➤ ¼ tsp. pepper
- ➤ ¼ C. grated Parmesan cheese
- ➤ ¼ C. mayonnaise
- ➤ 1 T. minced fresh parsley
- ➤ 1 T. lemon juice
- ➤ 2 T. sliced almonds

PREPARATION

Preheat the oven to 400°F. Place the butter in a 9 x 13" glass baking dish. Place the baking dish in the oven until the butter is melted. Meanwhile, chop the onion. Once the butter is melted, sprinkle the onion over the butter in the baking dish. Set the cod or haddock fillets over the onions. Sprinkle the seasoned salt, dillweed and pepper over the fish.

In a medium bowl, combine the Parmesan cheese, mayonnaise, parsley and lemon juice; mix until well combined. Spread the Parmesan mixture over the fish. Place the baking dish in the oven and bake, uncovered, for 18 to 20 minutes or until the fish flakes easily with a fork.

Meanwhile, toast the almonds. Arrange the almonds in an even layer on a baking sheet. Place the baking sheet in the oven on a rack above the baking dish with the fish. Bake the almonds for 6 to 8 minutes or until lightly browned.

To serve, place one baked fish fillet on each serving plate. Sprinkle ½ tablespoon of the toasted almonds over each serving.

★★★★ TACKLE BOX TRIVIA ★★★★

LEVEL HEADED

Fish is an important part of a healthy diet. Fish meat contains high-quality protein, other essential nutrients, omega-3 fatty acids, and is also low in saturated fat. However, you have probably heard that nearly all fish and shellfish contain traces of methylmercury, a mercury found in the water that can be harmful to the nervous system of unborn babies and young children. Fish with the highest levels of methylmercury are king mackerel, shark, swordfish and tilefish. These types of fish should be avoided by pregnant women, women who may become pregnant, nursing mothers and young children. Five of the most commonly eaten fish and shellfish that are low in mercury are shrimp, canned light tuna, salmon, pollock and catfish.

U.S. FOOD AND DRUG ADMINISTRATION

COOKING FISH & GAME

CHAPTER 2

Hunter's Reward

Hunting season brings with it a lot of excitement. Each year is another chance to bag the big one, try out your new gear and equipment and catch up with old friends.

Whether you're a novice or a seasoned hunter, there are always new things to learn about the preparation of wild game. And, while you may already have your tried-and-true favorites, each hunt can also be another chance to try a new recipe. Here, you'll find ideas and inspiration for ways to prepare everything from elk to rabbit, as well as handy tips and techniques to use while out on the hunt.

Hunting wild game is no easy task, and it can sometimes be intimidating to test something new with your hunted prize. When you shoot your prey and bring it home, you want to ensure that the best flavor will be brought forth in the preparation of your meal.

Now KICK OFF YOUR BOOTS, Sit Back, and COOK IT.

The recipes in this chapter are a collection of many decades' worth of testing, tasting, and re-testing in order to bring you meals that are sure to satisfy and keep you motivated for the next season. Enjoy the hunt and its bounty!

Whether you're out to bag a bird or a buck, remember that practice makes perfect. If you want to make a good clean shot in the field, practice shooting clay pigeons, a moving ground target, or even a stationary target to get the hang of shooting consistently.

DEER & ELK of North America

Just two species of deer are native to North America: the whitetail and mule deer. These species do occasionally interbreed. A third group, the Pacific coastal or blacktail deer, is simply a regional variation of the mule deer but is individual enough to be considered a subspecies. Other subspecies include the Sitka deer of Alaska, a close relative of the blacktail, plus the Coues deer of the Southwest United States and the Florida Keys deer, both of which are cousins to the whitetail.

Whitetail deer are most abundant in the eastern United States, though they can be found in each of the contiguous states. The only states without large populations of whitetail deer are California, Nevada and Utah. The whitetails' ability and willingness to live near humans make them the most commonly sighted, photographed and hunted large game animal.

Elk

Mule Deer

Whitetail Deer

TIPS ABOUT FIELD DRESSING & MORE:

- Pack your kill tag and hunting license together in a safe but accessible spot.
- When field dressing, wear disposable plastic gloves to reduce the risk of exposure to disease.
- Remove the entrails immediately. Avoid cutting the paunch and intestines since bacteria associated with food borne illness may be found in these organs.
- Clean your knife frequently with clean water, pre-moistened wipes or alcohol swabs to avoid dragging bacteria into the meat.

- Wipe out the cavity with paper towels and use a clean stick to prop open the cavity to aid with air circulation.
- If you wash the cavity with water, dry it quickly to prevent spoilage.
- Ice or snow packed in sealable plastic bags and placed in the cavity can aid with cooling. Be sure to keep the carcass out of direct sunlight.
- Cool the meat quickly to at least 35° to 40°F. Bacteria will multiply rapidly at temperatures from 41° to 140°F.

CUTS OF DEER MEAT

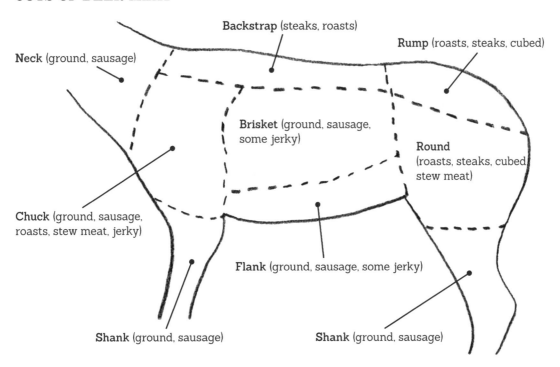

Backstrap (steaks, roasts)

Rump (roasts, steaks, cubed)

Neck (ground, sausage)

Brisket (ground, sausage, some jerky)

Round (roasts, steaks, cubed, stew meat)

Chuck (ground, sausage, roasts, stew meat, jerky)

Flank (ground, sausage, some jerky)

Shank (ground, sausage)

Shank (ground, sausage)

GRILLED VENISON STEAKS

Makes: 2 to 4 servings   **Prep Time:** 10 minutes plus 2 hours marinating   **Cook Time:** 8 to 14 minutes

INGREDIENTS

➤ 2 jalapeño peppers
➤ 1 C. butter or margarine
➤ ¼ C. lemon juice
➤ 2 tsp. salt
➤ 1 tsp. pepper
➤ 2 T. Worcestershire sauce
➤ 4 (12-oz.) venison tenderloin or round steaks

PREPARATION

Cut the jalapeño peppers into slices, removing any seeds. In a medium saucepan over medium-high heat, place the butter, lemon juice, salt, pepper, Worcestershire sauce and jalapeño slices. Bring the mixture to a boil. Remove from heat and let cool slightly.

Place the venison steaks in a square glass baking dish. Pour the marinade over the steaks. Cover the baking dish and place in the refrigerator for at least 30 minutes or up to 2 hours to marinate. The longer the steaks marinate, the stronger the flavor.

Meanwhile, preheat the grill. Remove the steaks from the refrigerator and discard the marinade. Grill the steaks over low heat or coals for approximately 4 to 7 minutes on each side, turning once, until the steaks are hot and grilled to desired doneness. If desired, baste steaks with additional lemon juice or Worcestershire sauce during or after grilling.

As shown by the variety of recipes in the section, venison can be prepared in any number of ways. If weather keeps you from grilling, try making a simple venison roast like the one shown here.

VENISON TENDERLOIN SANDWICHES

Makes: 4 large sandwiches   **Prep Time:** 5 minutes   **Cook Time:** 15 minutes

INGREDIENTS

- 2 large onions
- 2 (4-oz.) cans sliced mushrooms
- ¼ C. butter or margarine
- ¼ C. Worcestershire sauce
- 8 (12-oz.) venison tenderloin steaks, about ¾" thick
- ½ tsp. garlic powder
- ½ tsp. salt
- ¼ tsp. pepper
- 4 large hard rolls

PREPARATION

Cut the onions into slices and drain the mushrooms. In a large skillet over medium heat, sauté the onions and mushrooms in the butter and Worcestershire sauce.

Meanwhile, pound each venison steak to about ½" thickness. Add the tenderloins to the skillet. Cook the steaks for approximately 4 to 5 minutes on each side or to desired doneness. Sprinkle garlic powder, salt and pepper over the steaks while they are cooking.

To serve, split each hard roll in half and set open-faced on a plate. Place 2 steaks on the bottom half of each roll. Put a generous amount of the sautéed onions and mushrooms over the steaks. Replace the top half of each roll. Serve with any remaining sautéed onions or mushrooms on the side.

★★★★ BUCKSHOT BASICS ★★★★

IT'S A WRAP

1. To wrap your own meat for the freezer, you will need high-quality freezer paper. Ask your local butcher if you can purchase a roll of their paper.

2. Wrap the different cuts of meat separately and secure the package with freezer tape. If desired, you can double wrap the meat by wrapping the first package again with the inside package seam side down.

3. Try to force as much air out as possible from the package while you are wrapping.

4. Place the packages seam side up in the freezer.

BREADED VENISON STEAKS IN WINE SAUCE

Makes: 4 to 8 servings **Prep Time:** 15 minutes **Cook Time:** 1½ hours

INGREDIENTS

- 1 egg
- 1 sleeve round butter crackers
- ½ C. flour
- Salt and pepper
- 4 to 8 (12-oz.) venison round steaks
- 4 T. vegetable oil
- 1 onion
- 1 (4-oz.) can sliced mushrooms
- 1 C. red wine

PREPARATION

Preheat the oven to 350°F. In a small shallow bowl, beat the egg. Crush the crackers into fine crumbs and set them in a shallow dish. Add the flour, salt and pepper to the crushed crackers; mix well. Dip each venison steak first into the egg and then into the cracker mixture, turning to coat both sides.

In a large skillet over medium-high heat, heat the vegetable oil. Add the coated steaks to the hot oil, turning quickly to brown both sides. Only the outside of the steaks should be browned. Transfer the steaks to a glass baking dish.

Chop the onion and drain the mushrooms. Place the onions and mushrooms over the steaks in the baking dish. Pour the red wine over top. Cover the baking dish with aluminum foil. Bake for 1½ hours.

To serve, place one steak on each plate. Spoon some of the sauce, mushrooms and onions from the baking dish over each serving.

"Civilized life has altogether grown too tame, and, if it is to be stable, it must provide a harmless outlet for the impulses which our remote ancestors satisfied in hunting."

BERTRAND RUSSELL

VENISON STEAKS WITH CRANBERRY CHUTNEY

Makes: 4 servings   **Prep Time:** 15 minutes   **Cook Time:** 15 to 20 minutes plus 24 hours marinating

INGREDIENTS

- 4 (8-oz.) venison steaks
- 2 C. milk
- ¼ C. sour cream
- ¼ C. mayonnaise
- ¼ C. Major Grey's chutney*
- ¼ C. whole berry cranberry sauce
- 1 T. lemon juice
- 1 T. Dijon mustard
- 1 tsp. curry powder
- ½ tsp. cayenne pepper
- Olive oil
- Dry mustard powder
- Pepper
- ¼ C. butter or margarine, melted
- Salt and pepper

PREPARATION

Place the venison steaks in a square glass baking dish. Pour the milk over the steaks. Cover the baking dish and place in the refrigerator for 24 hours to marinate.

Meanwhile, prepare the chutney. In a large bowl, combine the sour cream, mayonnaise, Major Grey's chutney and cranberry sauce; mix until well combined. Add the lemon juice, Dijon mustard, curry powder and cayenne pepper, stirring until evenly incorporated. Cover the bowl and refrigerate the chutney for at least 1 hour or up to 24 hours. The flavors will blend more thoroughly the longer the chutney is refrigerated.

Preheat the grill to low heat or heat the broiler to low. To prepare the steaks, remove them from the refrigerator and discard the milk marinade. Rinse the steaks under cool water and pat them dry with a paper towel. Brush both sides of each steak with olive oil and sprinkle with dry mustard powder and pepper to coat.

Grill the steaks over low heat or coals, turning once, until the venison steaks are hot and grilled to desired doneness, about 5 minutes on each side. If using a broiler, broil the steaks for 3 to 4 minutes per side. Remove the steaks from the grill or broiler and quickly brush with the melted butter, then sprinkle with salt and pepper.

To serve, place one steak on each plate. Spoon a generous amount of the cranberry chutney sauce over each steak.

* Major Grey's is a type or style of mango chutney, not a brand name. You may use any brand of Major Grey's chutney. It makes a great addition to any kind of meat or salmon dish.

VENISON TIPS WITH SEASONED RICE & PEPPERS

Makes: 4 servings   **Prep Time:** 10 to 15 minutes   **Cook Time:** 20 minutes

INGREDIENTS

- 1 C. uncooked long-grain rice
- ½ C. uncooked broken vermicelli pasta
- 2 T. dried parsley flakes
- 3 T. beef bouillon granules
- 1 tsp. onion powder
- ¼ tsp. garlic powder
- ⅛ tsp. dried thyme
- 2 T. butter or margarine
- 1 small onion
- 1 green bell pepper
- 1 red bell pepper
- 1 T. vegetable oil
- 1 lb. cubed venison

PREPARATION

In a medium bowl, combine the rice, vermicelli, parsley flakes, beef bouillon, onion powder, garlic powder and thyme. Mix the ingredients together until evenly incorporated.

In a large heavy saucepan over medium-high heat, combine the butter and 2¼ cups water. Cover the saucepan and bring the water to a boil. Meanwhile, chop the onion and cut the peppers into thin strips.

Add the rice mixture, onion and peppers to the boiling water. Cover the saucepan and reduce the heat to medium-low. Allow the rice to simmer for 15 minutes or until the rice is tender.

Heat the vegetable oil in a large skillet over medium-high heat. Add the venison to the skillet; cook and stir until the venison is nicely browned on the outside and almost cooked through.

Add the browned venison to the rice while it is still simmering. Continue to simmer until the venison and peppers are tender. Toss rice, venison and peppers together with a fork. To serve, divide the rice mixture onto plates.

★★★★ SPORTSMAN COOKING ★★★★

GRILL MASTERS

Because of its low fat content, venison can stick to your grill. Be sure to brush the grate lightly with oil before the venison is set on the hot cooking surface. Also, the cooking time will be extremely important. Venison does not need to be cooked at the same high temperature as beef; it should be cooked to only about 145°F. Cooking to rare or medium-rare is ideal.

VENISON BARBECUE IN THE SLOW COOKER

Makes: 6 servings **Prep Time:** 15 minutes **Cook Time:** 10 hours

INGREDIENTS

- 1 medium onion
- 4 cloves garlic
- 3 lbs. cubed venison
- 1 C. red wine vinegar
- ½ C. Worcestershire sauce
- 2 tsp. tenderizing salt
- 2 tsp. seasoned salt
- 1 lb. bacon strips
- 2 C. ketchup
- ½ C. molasses
- ½ C. brown sugar

PREPARATION

Dice the onion and mince the garlic.

In a 5- or 6-quart slow cooker, place the onion, garlic, venison, red wine vinegar, Worcestershire sauce, tenderizing salt and seasoned salt. Cover the slow cooker and cook on high for 1 to 2 hours.

Meanwhile, in a large skillet over medium-high heat, cook the bacon strips until tender but not crispy. Remove the bacon from the skillet and chop into ½" pieces. After 1 or 2 hours, add the bacon, ketchup, molasses and brown sugar to the slow cooker. Cover the slow cooker and cook on low for 8 to 9 hours.

To serve, stir the ingredients in the slow cooker and transfer to serving plates. Serve with rice, potatoes or toast.

★★★★ SPORTSMAN COOKING ★★★★

COOKING WITH MOIST HEAT

Moist-heat cooking is a great way to tenderize tougher cuts of venison, such as shoulder roasts or stew meat. Using a slow-cooker, braising, and boiling in stew are all examples of cooking with moist heat.

COOKING FISH & GAME

HUNTER'S VENISON STEW

Makes: 6 hearty servings **Prep Time:** 15 minutes **Cook Time:** 30 to 45 minutes

INGREDIENTS

- 2 lbs. cubed venison
- 2 T. butter or margarine
- Salt and pepper
- 6 carrots
- 2 large potatoes
- 3 medium onions
- 3 stalks celery
- 1 (28-oz.) can crushed tomatoes

PREPARATION

In a large deep saucepan over medium-high heat, brown the venison in butter. Season the venison with salt and pepper to taste. Add 2 cups of water and continue to heat until the venison is tender, about 20 to 30 minutes.

Meanwhile, peel the carrots and potatoes. Cut the carrots, potatoes, onions and celery into small chunks. Add the vegetables and crushed tomatoes with juice to the venison in the saucepan. Continue to simmer until the potatoes are tender, about 15 minutes.

To serve, ladle the soup into bowls. Serve with crusty bread on the side.

★★★★ OPEN SEASON ★★★★

DEER MEAT YIELD

The average meat yield of a neck-shot mature buck compared to the meat yield of a domesticated animal, measured in pounds.

ANIMAL	WEIGHT*	MEAT	WASTE	% MEAT
Lamb**	50	40	10	80%
Hog	240	189	51	79%
Black Angus	600	438	162	73%
Holstein Steer	900	513	387	57%
Mature Buck	180	72	108	40%

* Carcass weight with head, hide and intestines removed
** Research performed by The University of Wisconsin

BUTCHER & PACKER, A SOURCE FOR BUTCHERING SUPPLIES AND INGREDIENTS

BROILED VENISON PATTIES

Makes: 12 small patties or 6 large   **Prep Time:** 10 to 15 minutes   **Cook Time:** 5 to 10 minutes

INGREDIENTS
- 2 T. butter or margarine
- ½ small onion
- 2 T. chopped celery leaves
- 1 tsp. dried parsley flakes
- ¾ lb. ground venison
- ½ C. finely crushed crackers
- ¼ C. milk
- 1 egg
- 1 T. flour
- 2 tsp. lemon juice
- Dash of garlic powder
- Dash of pepper

PREPARATION
In a small saucepan over medium-high heat, melt the butter. Chop the onion. Add the onion, celery leaves and parsley flakes to the saucepan; sauté until tender. Transfer the sautéed onion mixture to a medium bowl.

To the bowl, add the venison, crackers, milk, egg, flour, lemon juice, garlic powder and pepper. Mix by hand until well combined.

Shape the mixture into patties of desired size. Fry the patties in a skillet over medium-high heat until browned or place under an oven broiler for 2 to 3 minutes on each side.

★★★★ SPORTSMAN COOKING ★★★★

HANDLE WITH CARE

Handle ground venison very gently when shaping into patties. Too much handling will cause the patties or burgers to have a compact texture. When frying, grilling or broiling, gently turn the patties only once.

BARBECUED VENISON MEATBALLS

Makes: About 20 (1") meatballs **Prep Time:** 10 minutes plus 2 hours marinating
Cook Time: 1 hour and 15 minutes

INGREDIENTS

- 1 egg
- 1½ lbs. ground venison
- ½ C. dry bread crumbs
- 1 tsp. salt
- Pepper
- 1 C. ketchup
- 1 T. Worcestershire sauce
- 2 T. brown sugar
- 2 T. vinegar
- ¼ tsp. salt
- Dash of pepper

If your deer or elk has a spectacular display of antlers, you might want to preserve them for mounting. Preserve the velvet on antlers by making small incisions at each antler tip. Then, suspend the antlers with tips down and inject them with formaldehyde or a similar chemical, The resulting solution will drain from the incisions.

PREPARATION

Using a fork, lightly whisk the egg in the bottom of a large bowl. Add the venison, bread crumbs, salt and pepper to taste. Mix by hand until well combined. Shape the mixture into 1" meatballs. Place the meatballs in a 9 x 13" glass baking dish.

In a medium bowl, combine the ketchup, Worcestershire sauce, brown sugar, vinegar, salt and pepper. Mix the sauce ingredients together and pour over the meatballs in the baking dish. Cover the baking dish with aluminum foil and place the meatballs and sauce in the refrigerator for at least 2 hours or up to 24 hours.

Preheat the oven to 350°F. Place the covered dish in the oven and bake the meatballs for 1 hour and 15 minutes, basting once or twice with the sauce from the bottom of the dish.

To serve, spoon the meatballs and sauce onto serving plates. This dish pairs well with rice, pasta or potatoes.

"If Elvis Presley had been a bow hunter, he'd probably be alive today."

— TED NUGENT

VENISON MEATLOAF WITH A KICK

Makes: 4 servings **Prep Time:** 15 minutes **Cook Time:** 50 minutes

INGREDIENTS

- 8 saltine crackers
- 1 egg
- 1 lb. ground venison
- 1 T. brown sugar
- ½ tsp. spicy brown mustard
- ¼ tsp. dried cilantro
- ½ tsp. garlic powder
- ½ tsp. dried onion flakes
- ¼ tsp. ground thyme
- Dash of ground cinnamon
- Dash of paprika
- 3 T. ketchup
- 1 T. brown sugar

PREPARATION

Preheat the oven to 350°F. Crush the saltine crackers and lightly beat the egg.

In a large bowl, combine the crackers, egg, venison and 1 tablespoon of brown sugar; mix by hand until well combined. Add the mustard, cilantro, garlic powder, onion flakes, thyme, cinnamon and paprika. Mix again by hand until all ingredients are well combined and evenly incorporated.

Lightly pat the mixture into a 5 x 9" loaf pan or 9" square baking dish. Bake uncovered for 40 minutes or until the internal temperature of the meatloaf registers 160°F on a meat thermometer.

Meanwhile, in a medium bowl, combine the ketchup and remaining 1 tablespoon of brown sugar; mix well. After the loaf has baked for 40 minutes, spread the ketchup mixture evenly over top. Return the loaf to the oven for an additional 10 minutes.

To serve, remove the loaf from the oven and let it cool in the pan for 5 minutes before cutting into slices or squares.

★★★★ BUCKSHOT BASICS ★★★★

PREPPED FOR PREP

1. Before cooking, thoroughly defrost venison in original wrapping.

2. Once the original package has been opened, do not use plastic wrap to cover the meat, as this could make it sweat. It is undesirable for meat to sweat before it is cooked as this will release moisture and make the cooked meat tougher.

3. Slice meat across the grain, not with it.

4. Allow at least 4 to 5 ounces of meat per serving.

5. Because of its leanness, be careful not to overcook venison. Always cook venison rare or medium-rare, as it can be tough and dry when well-done.

DEER CAMP VENISON CHILI

Makes: 10 to 12 servings **Prep Time:** 10 to 15 minutes **Cook Time:** 25 minutes to 1 hour

INGREDIENTS

- 1 large onion
- 6 stalks celery
- 4 jalapeño peppers
- 2 lbs. ground venison
- 1 T. crushed red pepper flakes
- 1 (40-oz.) can hot chili beans
- 4 (14½-oz.) cans Italian-style stewed tomatoes
- 1 (6-oz.) can tomato paste
- 1 tsp. salt
- White pepper

PREPARATION

Chop the onion and celery. Slice the jalapeño peppers and carefully remove and discard the seeds.

In a large deep soup pot over medium-high heat, brown the venison, adding a little vegetable oil if necessary. Add the onion, celery, jalapeños and red pepper flakes; continue to sauté until the onions are transparent, about 2 to 3 minutes.

Drain the chili beans. Add the stewed tomatoes with juice, tomato paste and chili beans to the pot; stir well. Continue to heat, stirring often. Add the salt and white pepper to taste. Reduce the heat to low and let the chili simmer until ready to serve. If the chili is too spicy, stir in 1 to 2 tablespoons of sugar.

To serve, ladle the chili into bowls. Some nice garnishes are a dollop of sour cream, a few corn chips and sliced green onions.

"Pa did not like a country so old and worn out that the hunting was poor. He wanted to go west. For two years he had wanted to go west and take a homestead, but Ma did not want to leave the settled country."

— LAURA INGALLS WILDER

HERBED VENISON ROAST
WITH RAISINBERRY RELISH

Makes: 4 servings per pound of roast   **Prep Time:** 25 minutes
Cook Time: 15 minutes per pound, 1 hour for a 4-pound roast

INGREDIENTS

- 2¼ C. golden raisins
- 2 C. orange juice
- ½ C. sugar
- ¼ C. lemon juice
- 3 C. fresh or frozen cranberries
- 1 T. grated orange peel
- 1 (2- to 4-lb.) venison shoulder roast
- 1 to 2 T. dried provencal herbs*
- ½ to 1 lb. bacon strips

* Provencal herbs, or Herbes de Provence, is a mixture of dried basil, thyme, rosemary, oregano, sage and marjoram. If this seasoning is not available, any combination of these herbs can be used as a substitute.

PREPARATION

Preheat the oven to 500°F. Begin by preparing the raisinberry relish. In a medium saucepan over medium-high heat, combine the golden raisins, orange juice, sugar, lemon juice and 1 cup water. Increase heat to high and bring the liquid to a boil, stirring to dissolve the sugar. Once the sugar is completely dissolved, reduce the heat to medium and allow the liquid to simmer for 10 minutes. Add the cranberries and orange peel. Simmer for an additional 10 minutes or until the liquid is reduced so that it barely covers the raisins and cranberries. Remove relish from heat and let cool.

Remove 1 cup of the relish mixture from the saucepan and puree in a blender or food processor. Set aside the remaining relish for serving with the roast.

Rub all sides of the roast with the provencal herbs. Wrap the roast with overlapping bacon strips and tie with kitchen string or drape the strips of bacon over the roast. Place the roast on a rack in a shallow roasting pan. Brush the pureed relish over the bacon-wrapped roast. Place the roasting pan in the preheated oven and reduce the temperature to 400°F. Roast uncovered for 15 minutes per pound.

To serve, slice the roast across the grain. Transfer slices to serving plates and garnish with the reserved raisinberry relish.

★★★★ SPORTSMAN COOKING ★★★★

SELF-BASTING

When you're preparing a venison roast, remember to baste often with the pan juices so the meat will not dry out. Or, for a self-basting method, drape overlapping bacon strips around the roast as a way to enclose the juices in the meat. If necessary, secure the bacon strips by wrapping kitchen string around the roast.

SLOW-COOKED ITALIAN VENISON ROAST

Makes: 4 servings per pound **Prep Time:** 15 minutes plus 8 hours marinating
Cook Time: 45 minutes per pound, 3 hours for a 4-pound roast

INGREDIENTS

- 1 (4- to 5-lb.) venison roast
- 1 (16-oz.) bottle Italian dressing
- 2 T. flour
- ½ to 1 lb. bacon strips
- 2 green bell peppers
- 2 medium onions
- 1 (4-oz.) can sliced mushrooms
- 1 (10½-oz.) can French onion soup

PREPARATION

Place the venison roast in a large pot or bowl. Pour Italian dressing over roast, turning to coat all sides. Cover the pot and place roast in refrigerator for 8 hours or overnight to marinate.

Preheat the oven to 280°F. Remove the roast from the pot and place on a rack in a roasting pan. Pour any remaining marinade dressing from the pot into a jar. Add the flour to the jar and shake well. Place the jar in the refrigerator.

Wrap the roast with overlapping bacon strips and tie with kitchen string or drape the strips of bacon over the roast. Cut the green bell peppers and onions into chunks. Drain the mushrooms. Spread the vegetables around the roast and pour the French onion soup over the roast. Cover the roasting pan. Roast for 45 minutes per pound.

To serve, remove the roast from the pan and slice the roast across the grain. Drain the drippings from the roasting pan into a small saucepan over medium-high heat. Bring the drippings to a boil and stir in the flour mixture from the jar. Continue to boil and mix well to make a thick gravy. Pour gravy over roast or individual servings.

★★★★ **BUCKSHOT BASICS** ★★★★

SAFE MARINATING & SAUCE PREP

Sauce that is used to marinate raw meat, poultry or seafood should not be used on cooked foods unless it is boiled before applying. The raw meat, poultry or seafood may have illness-causing bacteria present on the surface, which could contaminate the marinade. Bring the marinade to a rolling boil to kill any pathogens that may be present.

THE IOWA STATE UNIVERSITY EXTENSION OFFICE

OVEN-BAKED VENISON SAUSAGE

Makes: About 10 servings   **Prep Time:** 15 minutes plus 24 hours chilling   **Cook Time:** 1 hour and 20 minutes

INGREDIENTS

- ➤ 2 lbs. ground venison
- ➤ 2 T. liquid smoke flavoring
- ➤ ¼ tsp. garlic powder
- ➤ 1 tsp. mustard seed
- ➤ ⅛ tsp. pepper
- ➤ ½ tsp. onion salt
- ➤ 2 T. tenderizing salt

PREPARATION

In a large bowl, combine the venison, liquid smoke flavoring, garlic powder, mustard seed, pepper and onion salt. Add 1 cup of water and the tenderizing salt. Mix all ingredients by hand until well combined.

Place a 12 x 18" length of aluminum foil on a flat surface, shiny side up. Shape the venison mixture into a log of desired-size thickness. Place the log on the aluminum foil and wrap tightly, securing the ends. Place the wrapped log in the refrigerator for at least 24 hours.

Preheat the oven to 325°F. Pierce holes in the bottom of the aluminum foil and set the wrapped log on a jellyroll pan or baking sheet with an edge. Bake for 1 hour and 20 minutes. Carefully remove the wrapped log and let cool for 10 minutes before placing in the refrigerator to chill for at least 24 hours before slicing.

To serve, slice the sausage, cutting through the aluminum foil. Peel the aluminum foil off each slice before eating.

★★★★ HUNTSMAN'S HINT ★★★★

BIG SHOT

It is important to take a good shot in the field. The "gaminess" of venison is directly related to how much the deer runs after being hit. A panicked deer will flood its body with adrenaline as the heart races and blood pours into the muscles. The extra blood helps rev up the muscles for flight but produces lactic and pyruvic acids in return, which is a major reason why venison can sometimes taste gamey.

SPICED WINE VENISON SAUSAGE

Makes: About 15 servings   **Prep Time:** 15 minutes plus 3 days chilling   **Cook Time:** 4 to 6 hours

INGREDIENTS

- 3½ lbs. ground venison
- 1½ lbs. lard or beef tallow
- 3½ T. tenderizing salt
- ¾ C. Burgundy wine
- 2 T. sugar
- 2 T. mustard seed
- 1 T. onion powder
- 1½ tsp. coriander
- 1½ tsp. minced fresh gingerroot
- ½ tsp. ground nutmeg
- 1½ tsp. garlic powder
- 1½ tsp. pepper
- Sausage casings

PREPARATION

In a large bowl, combine the ground venison, lard or tallow, and tenderizing salt, mixing thoroughly by hand for 5 minutes. Cover the bowl and chill in the refrigerator for 3 days, mixing twice each day.

On the fourth day, in a medium bowl, combine the Burgundy wine, sugar, mustard seed, onion powder, coriander, gingerroot, nutmeg, garlic powder and pepper; mix well. Add the wine mixture to the meat and mix until well combined.

Stuff the mixture into the sausage casings. Using a smoker, smoke the sausage over hickory chips at 160°F for 4 hours. Increase the temperature to 180°F and continue to smoke until the sausage reaches 160°F on a meat thermometer. Chill the sausage in the refrigerator for 24 hours before slicing and serving.

★★★★ SPORTSMAN COOKING ★★★★

A CASE FOR CASINGS

If you are preparing your own venison sausage and plan to use a smoker, you will need sausage casings. The two main types of casings for venison are natural or synthetic. Natural casings are made from cleaned intestinal membranes of cows, hogs, lambs and sheep. Synthetic casings are available in cellulosic (soluble cotton linters), collagen (animal bones and cartilage), fibrous (formulated polymers) or muslin (fine-weave cotton fabric). For venison sausage, natural pork casings or fibrous synthetic casings are desirable and available from many hunting stores and online suppliers.

VENISON JERKY

Makes: Each of the marinades on pages 86 and 87 marinates 3 pounds of venison jerky strips

PREPARATION

Cut the venison into long, evenly-thin strips.*

In a medium bowl, combine the liquid and/or seasoning marinade ingredients. Add venison strips and mix until the strips are completely covered in marinade or seasonings. Cover the bowl and place in the refrigerator for 1 hour to marinate.

Dehydrator: Program the dehydrator to a setting of 160°F. Place marinated venison strips on the dehydrator racks and close tightly. Turn on dehydrator and dry jerky strips for 8 to 10 hours, turning at least once halfway through drying time.

Oven: Remove all oven racks and place one rack in the lowest position. Set a large baking sheet on the lowest rack. Preheat the oven to 200°F. Use toothpicks and one of the removed oven racks to create hanging supports for the jerky strips. Drape the marinated strips over the toothpicks and suspend the toothpicks between the bars of the rack. Return the rack to the oven. Cook for 2 to 3 hours, sampling for desired doneness after every hour.

Grill or Smoker: Cook the marinated strips at 200°F over indirect heat for 1 to 2 hours, sampling for desired doneness every 30 minutes.

Jerky makes a delicious snack, but you want to make sure it's healthy to enjoy. Freeze any meat you plan to use for jerky completely to destroy any existing parasites.

* The U.S. Department of Agriculture recommends that jerky made from beef or venison be steamed, roasted or boiled to 160°F before drying.

★★★★ HUNTSMAN'S HINT ★★★★

WEIGHING IN

You can get a pretty good estimate of a live deer's weight by multiplying the field-dressed weight by 1.28. Though the number will not be exact, it will provide a ball park figure for informal comparisons.

JERKY MARINADES

Basic Recipe
- ⅓ C. garlic salt
- ⅓ C. onion salt
- ⅓ C. pepper
- ⅓ C. salt
- 1 C. Worcestershire sauce

Smokey
- 1 T. liquid smoke flavoring
- ¾ C. soy sauce
- ¾ C. Worcestershire sauce
- 3 T. ketchup
- ¼ to ½ tsp. pepper
- ¾ tsp. garlic powder
- ¾ tsp. salt

Kickin' Spiced
- 1 C. soy sauce
- ½ C. lime juice
- ½ C. vinegar
- ¼ C. crushed red pepper flakes
- 2 T. garlic powder

Oriental
- 2 T. salt
- 2 T. pepper
- 1 large onion, minced
- 5 cloves garlic, pressed
- 1 C. brown sugar
- ⅓ C. soy sauce
- 1¼ C. red wine
- 1½ C. pineapple juice

★★★★ OPEN SEASON ★★★★

LIVING LARGE

An average cow elk weighs more than 500 pounds, stands 4½ feet at the shoulder and measures 6½ feet from nose to rump. An average bull elk weighs about 700 pounds, stands 5 feet at the shoulder and measures more than 8 feet from nose to rump.

Baja-Style

- 2 T. salt
- 2 T. pepper
- 2 T. coriander
- 1½ tsp. chili powder
- 1½ tsp. ground ginger
- 1½ tsp. ground turmeric
- 1½ tsp. ground cumin

Spicy Garlic

- 1 T. salt
- ¾ tsp. cracked pepper
- ¾ tsp. cayenne pepper
- 1 T. onion powder
- 6 cloves garlic, minced
- 6 T. tangy barbecue sauce
- ½ C. Worcestershire sauce
- 1½ tsp. paprika

Mild Mexican

- 1 T. salt
- ¾ tsp. pepper
- 1 T. chili powder
- 1½ tsp. garlic powder
- 1½ tsp. dried oregano
- 1 T. paprika

Tangy Seasoned

- ½ C. lemon juice
- 1 small onion, minced
- ¼ C. brown sugar
- 2 tsp. liquid smoke flavoring
- 1 T. seasoned salt
- ¼ tsp. pepper
- 3 bay leaves, crushed

Western BBQ

- 1 T. salt
- 6 T. brown sugar
- ¾ tsp. pepper
- 1 C. red wine vinegar
- ½ tsp. cayenne pepper
- 1 C. ketchup
- 1 T. onion powder
- 1½ tsp. garlic powder
- 1 T. dry mustard powder

SKILLET CORNBREAD ELK CASSEROLE

Makes: 4 to 6 servings   **Prep Time:** 10 minutes   **Cook Time:** 30 minutes

INGREDIENTS

- 8 to 10 bacon strips
- 1 medium onion
- 2 lbs. ground elk meat
- 2 (15-oz.) cans whole kernel corn
- 2 (10¾-oz.) cans tomato soup
- 1 tsp. garlic powder
- 1 (1¼-oz.) pkg. chili seasoning
- 2 (8½-oz.) boxes corn muffin mix
- 1 egg
- ⅓ C. milk

PREPARATION

Preheat the oven to 350°F. In a large oven-safe skillet over medium-high heat, cook the bacon strips. Remove the bacon strips to paper towels to drain, reserving the drippings in the skillet. Crumble the bacon.

Chop the onion. Add the onion and elk meat to the drippings in the skillet. Heat, stirring often, until the onions are tender and the meat is browned. Pour the drippings from the skillet, retaining the onions and meat in the skillet. Reduce the heat to medium. Drain the corn. Add the corn, tomato soup, garlic powder, chili seasoning and bacon to the skillet.

In a medium bowl, combine corn muffin mix, egg and milk. Mix until well combined. Spread the cornbread batter over the ingredients in the skillet. Place the skillet in the oven and bake for 15 to 20 minutes or until the cornbread topping is golden brown.

★★★★ TWELVE-POINT FACT ★★★★

WASTE NOT

Native Americans hunted elk for hundreds of years. In addition to eating elk meat, they put the rest of the carcass to good use. The bones and antlers were made into weapons such as bows and clubs. The hides were made into war shields as well as robes, moccasins and tipi covers. Even the teeth were utilized—for necklaces and clothing decoration.

ALL ABOUT HUNTING DOGS

The story of man and his dog is a classic that never gets old. A good dog can be your companion at home and on the lake or in the woods. If you are fond of friends of the four-legged variety, the following might interest you.

BEST BREEDS

A hunting trip is not complete without man's best friend. Here are some of the top hunting dogs to help you bag your game:

- Basset Hound
- Beagle
- Bloodhound
- Boykin Spaniel
- Brittany
- Cairn Terrier
- Chesapeake Bay Retriever
- Cocker Spaniel
- Coonhound
- Daschund
- English Setter
- English Springer Spaniel
- Fox Terrier
- German Shorthaired Pointer
- Golden Retriever
- Irish Setter
- Labrador Retriever
- Pointer
- Spanish Water Dog
- Weimaraner

BEST NAMES

When it comes to your pet, it's all in the name, and when it comes to your hunting companion, you'll want a name as rough and rugged as the great outdoors. Here are some ideas to get you started.

- Ammo
- Apollo
- Bailey
- Bear
- Buck or Buckshot
- Bo
- Bullet
- Chase
- Cujo
- Dakota
- Dixie
- Drake
- Duke
- General
- Gunner
- Jag
- Kody
- Magnum
- Pistol
- Rambo
- Reload
- Scout
- Trigger
- Trapper
- Winchester
- Zeke
- Zeus

A well-trained hunting dog can make an excellent addition to your hunting crew.

ELK & PEPPER STIR-FRY

Makes: 4 servings   **Prep Time:** 15 minutes plus 30 minutes marinating   **Cook Time:** 15 minutes

INGREDIENTS

- 1 (1 lb.) elk steak, thinly sliced
- ½ C. soy sauce
- 1 T. cornstarch
- ¼ C. peanut oil
- 4 medium tomatoes
- 1 green bell pepper
- ¼ C. peanut oil
- ¾ C. chicken broth
- ¼ C. dry sherry
- 1 T. cornstarch

PREPARATION

Place the sliced elk meat in a large bowl. Pour the soy sauce over the elk and sprinkle with cornstarch; mix lightly. Cover the bowl and place in the refrigerator for at least 30 minutes and up to 24 hours to marinate.

Remove the elk from the refrigerator and discard the marinade. Place the peanut oil in a large skillet over medium-high heat. Once the oil is hot, place the elk strips in the skillet and heat, stirring often, until the strips are browned on all sides and almost cooked through. Remove the strips and drippings to a plate and keep warm.

Meanwhile, chop the tomatoes and cut the green pepper into thin strips. Add another ¼ cup peanut oil to the skillet over medium-high heat. Add the tomatoes and heat for 1 minute, stirring constantly. Place 1 tablespoon of the chicken broth in a small glass. Add the remaining chicken broth to the skillet. Stir in the pepper strips and cooked elk strips with drippings. Mix in the sherry and stir well.

Add 1 tablespoon of cornstarch to the reserved chicken broth in the small glass; mix well. Push the steak and vegetables to one side of the skillet and slowly pour the cornstarch mixture into the liquid in the pan. Mix lightly and bring to a boil to thicken, stirring constantly. Mix all ingredients together, adding more soy sauce as desired. If desired, serve over hot cooked rice.

"No, I'm not a good shot, but I shoot often."

— TEDDY ROOSEVELT

GRILLED ELK CHOPS

Makes: 8 to 10 servings **Prep Time:** 10 minutes **Cook Time:** 25 to 35 minutes

INGREDIENTS

- 10 elk chops
- 1 large onion
- 4 cloves garlic
- 6 oz. beer
- ¼ C. butter or margarine
- Garlic salt

PREPARATION

Use disposable aluminum foil pans or create your own. Use a double layer of heavy-duty foil and mold it over an upside-down pan or large rectangular baking dish. Leave extra length at all edges, fold them over and crimp well for strength.

Preheat an outdoor grill to medium-high heat. Place the elk chops in the pans. Chop the onion and mince the garlic. Sprinkle the onion and garlic over the elk chops. Pour the beer over the chops. Cut the butter into pats and place on top of the chops. Place the pan on the grate and cover the grill.

When the elk chops are cooked through, after about 20 to 30 minutes, remove them from the pan. Discard the pan and all the drippings. Return the elk chops to the hot grill and sprinkle with garlic salt. Grill for 2 minutes on each side, sprinkling with more garlic salt.

★★★★ TWELVE-POINT FACT ★★★★

ACTING ELK

- When alarmed, elk will raise their heads high, open their eyes wide, move stiffly and rotate their ears to listen.

- Agitated elk will hold their heads high, lay their ears back, flare their nostrils, and sometimes even punch with their front hooves.

- If a harem cow wanders from the herd, a bull will stretch his neck out low, tip up his nose, tilt his antlers back and circle her.

- Elk threaten each other by curling back their upper lips, grinding their teeth and hissing softly.

PHEASANT, QUAIL & MORE

Pheasant

California Quail

Quail

Partridge

Grouse

TIPS ABOUT FIELD DRESSING & MORE:

- Two common mistakes in handling shot birds are stacking birds together in the closed trunk of a car on a hot day or carrying several birds in a hot, rubber-lined game pocket. Both of these practices will cause an undesirable loss of quality in the meat.

- Cool the body heat from the birds as quickly as possible, keeping the temperature down until the birds are cleaned.

- Pull out the feathers from below the breast bone to the anal opening. Next, make a cut through the skin and muscle, starting below the breastbone and continuing down to the anal opening. Reach in and remove the internal organs, pulling down toward the anal opening. Be sure to remove the windpipe and crop.

- Some hunters prefer to pack the empty cavity with dry grass to absorb blood and prevent flies from crawling in the cavity during warm weather.

- Once home, pluck or skin the birds. Plucking takes longer, but removing the skin and fat will also remove a lot of the flavor. An exception to this rule is the mature sage grouse and some types of waterfowl for which removing the skin makes the meat more palatable.

SINGLE BONELESS PIECES OF MEAT PRODUCED FROM ONE PHEASANT

meat from two drumsticks or legs

two thighs

two breast halves

PHEASANT STUFFED WITH WILD RICE DRESSING

Makes: 4 to 6 servings   **Prep Time:** 20 minutes   **Cook Time:** 2½ hours

INGREDIENTS

- 2 whole pheasants, cleaned
- 1 C. wild rice
- 1 tsp. salt
- ½ small onion
- ½ green bell pepper
- 1 stalk celery
- 1 (4-oz.) can chopped mushrooms
- ¼ tsp. pepper
- 4 bacon strips
- ½ C. butter or margarine, melted

PREPARATION

Wipe the plucked and cleaned pheasants, inside and out, with a damp cloth.

Bring 1 quart of water to a boil in a large saucepan over medium-high heat. Add the wild rice and salt. Reduce the heat to low, cover the saucepan and let the rice simmer for 40 minutes.

Meanwhile, mince the onion, green bell pepper and celery. Drain the chopped mushrooms.

Preheat the oven to 325°F. After 40 minutes, drain any unabsorbed water from the rice and spread the rice onto paper towels to dry. Transfer the cooked, dry rice to a medium bowl and add the onion, green bell pepper and celery. Add the mushrooms and season with the pepper; mix well. Stuff the pheasants with the wild rice dressing.

Place the stuffed pheasants, breast side up, on a rack in a roasting pan. Drape two strips of bacon over each pheasant breast. Roast in the oven for about 2½ hours or until the pheasant is tender. Baste the pheasants every 30 minutes with the melted butter and pan drippings.

To serve, place the pheasants on a platter. Remove the stuffing from the pheasants and transfer to a baking dish. If the stuffing registers below 165°F on a meat thermometer, return the dish to the oven until the temperature of the stuffing reaches at least 165°F. Carve the pheasants and serve with the wild rice stuffing on the side.

★★★★ SPORTSMAN COOKING ★★★★

STUFF ABOUT STUFFING

Stuffing cooked inside a turkey or other bird should be cooked to a minimum temperature of 165°F. Stuffing is often undercooked because many cooks do not allow for the extra cooking time required for a stuffed bird (typically another hour for large birds). Undercooking stuffing, especially stuffing containing meat, can increase the chances of food poisoning.

RED CURRANT ROASTED PHEASANT

Makes: 2 to 3 servings   **Prep Time:** 15 minutes   **Cook Time:** 1 to 1½ hours

INGREDIENTS

- 1 whole pheasant, cleaned
- 1 apple
- ½ lb. ground sausage
- 1 egg
- 1 tsp. dried parsley flakes
- ½ tsp. salt
- ½ tsp. pepper
- 2 T. red currant jelly
- 2 bacon strips
- ¼ C. butter or margarine
- ½ to 1 C. sherry wine
- 1 T. red currant jelly
- Juice of ½ lemon

PREPARATION

Wipe the plucked and cleaned pheasant, inside and out, with a damp cloth.

Preheat the oven to 350°F. Core and chop the apple. In a medium bowl, combine the apple, sausage, egg, parsley flakes, salt, pepper and 2 tablespoons of red currant jelly; mix well. Stuff the pheasant with the sausage and apple stuffing.

Place the stuffed pheasant, breast side up, on a rack in a roasting pan. Drape the strips of bacon over the pheasant breast. Roast the pheasant in the oven for 45 minutes.

Meanwhile, in a medium saucepan over low heat, combine the butter, sherry, 1 tablespoon of red currant jelly and lemon juice. Heat, stirring often, until the sauce is melted and smooth.

Remove the pheasant from the oven after 45 minutes; drain and discard the drippings from the pan. Pour the melted butter and sherry sauce over the pheasant. Return the pheasant to the oven for an additional 15 to 30 minutes, or until the pheasant is tender. Baste every 10 minutes with the sauce in the pan.

To serve, place the pheasant on a platter. Remove the stuffing from the pheasant and transfer to a baking dish. If the stuffing registers below 165°F on a meat thermometer, return the dish to the oven until the temperature of the stuffing reaches at least 165°F. Carve the pheasant and serve with the sausage and apple stuffing on the side.

"When you have shot one bird flying, you have shot all birds flying. They are all different and they fly in different ways, but the sensation is the same and the last one is as good as the first."

— ERNEST HEMINGWAY, *Winner Take Nothing*

SAUTÉED QUAIL WITH MUSHROOMS

Makes: 4 servings   **Prep Time:** 15 minutes   **Cook Time:** 35 to 40 minutes

INGREDIENTS

- 4 whole quail, cleaned
- 2 lemons
- Salt and pepper
- ¼ C. butter or margarine
- 1 (16 oz.) pkg. whole fresh mushrooms
- ½ C. white wine
- Fresh parsley sprigs

PREPARATION

Wipe the plucked and cleaned quail, inside and out, with a damp cloth.

Cut each lemon in half. Rub the cut side of one lemon half over each quail. Season the inside and outside of each quail with salt and pepper.

In a large skillet over medium-high heat, melt the butter. Add the quail and mushrooms to the skillet. Brown the quail on all sides while sautéing the mushrooms.

Once the quail are nicely browned, add the white wine and several fresh parsley sprigs. Cover the skillet and simmer for 15 to 20 minutes or until the quail are tender.

To serve, place each quail on a serving plate. Discard any wilted parsley sprigs. Spoon the mushrooms and sauce from the skillet over each quail. Garnish with fresh parsley sprigs.

Quail is a favorite ingredient for many restaurant chefs and home cooks because the flavor works in harmony with several types of sauces and seasonings. Quail is also a popular choice because, in addition to being meaty and flavorful, it's nutritious. Quail meat is higher in protein and lower in fat and calories than chicken or turkey.

PHEASANT BREAST WITH PEACH GLAZE

Makes: 2 to 4 servings   **Prep Time:** 20 minutes   **Cook Time:** 1 hour and 5 minutes

INGREDIENTS

- ➢ 2 whole pheasant breasts
- ➢ ¼ C. butter or margarine, melted
- ➢ Salt and pepper
- ➢ Paprika
- ➢ 1 (15-oz.) can peach halves in syrup
- ➢ ½ C. sugar
- ➢ 3 T. brandy
- ➢ Dash of ground cinnamon or nutmeg

PREPARATION

Preheat the oven to 350°F. Brush the pheasant breasts with the melted butter. Season both sides of each breast with salt and pepper; dust with paprika. Tightly wrap each pheasant breast separately in a sheet of aluminum foil. Place the wrapped pheasant breasts on a baking sheet and place in the oven; bake for 1 hour.

Meanwhile, prepare the glaze. In a blender, place four of the canned peach halves. Add ¼ cup of the liquid syrup from the canned peaches to the blender. Set aside any remaining peach halves or syrup for another use. To the blender, add the sugar, brandy and a dash of cinnamon or nutmeg. Place the lid on the blender and process until blended and smooth. Pour the blended peach mixture into a medium saucepan over medium heat. Bring the peach glaze to a boil and remove from heat.

After 1 hour, remove the pheasant breasts from the oven and carefully open the aluminum packets. Brush a generous amount of the peach glaze over each pheasant breast. Keeping the aluminum packets open, return the pheasant breasts to the oven for 5 minutes.

To serve, drizzle the remaining peach glaze over the serving plates. Place one pheasant breast or pheasant breast half over the sauce on each plate.

★★★★ OPEN SEASON ★★★★

PRICELESS

Each year, an average of about $120 billion is spent to pursue wildlife-related recreation, including hunting, fishing, observation and photography. This spending equates to about 1% of gross domestic product, which means that one out of every one hundred dollars of all goods and services produced in the United States is associated with wildlife recreation.

THE NATIONAL SURVEY OF HUNTING, FISHING, AND WILDLIFE-ASSOCIATED RECREATION

BAKED CAJUN PHEASANT BREASTS

Makes: 2 to 4 servings   **Prep Time:** 10 minutes   **Cook Time:** 1 hour and 10 minutes

INGREDIENTS

- ➤ 1 (5½-oz.) box Cajun flavored coating mix
- ➤ 2 whole pheasant breasts
- ➤ 1 medium onion
- ➤ 1 (4-oz.) can sliced mushrooms
- ➤ 2 (6-oz.) boxes long grain and wild rice mix
- ➤ 1 (10¾-oz.) can cream of mushroom soup
- ➤ 1 (10¾-oz.) can cream of celery soup
- ➤ 1 (16-oz.) pkg. shredded cheddar cheese

PREPARATION

Preheat the oven to 375°F. Place the Cajun coating mix in a large shallow dish. Cut each pheasant breast in half and roll in the coating mix, turning to coat both sides.

Chop the onion. Place the onion and seasoned pheasant breast halves in a large skillet over medium-high heat. Cook until the pheasant breast halves are browned, turning once, and until the onion is soft and transparent.

Drain the mushrooms. In a medium bowl, combine the mushrooms, wild rice mix, cream of mushroom soup and cream of celery soup. Add 1¼ cups water and mix everything together until well combined.

In a 9 x 13" glass baking dish, place the pheasant breast halves and onions. Pour the rice and soup mixture evenly over the pheasant and onions. Place the uncovered baking dish in the oven and bake for 1 hour.

After 1 hour, remove the baking dish from the oven and sprinkle the shredded cheddar cheese over top. Return to the oven for an additional 5 to 10 minutes or until the cheese is completely melted.

To serve, place one pheasant breast half on each serving plate and spoon some of the rice and onions over each serving.

Sometimes the best way to catch pheasants is to work with a partner. A good hunting dog, with its natural instincts and senses, will certainly help you find and catch game, but you can also work with other hunters. Pheasants can be ambushed by a group of hunters waiting in hiding as another hunter drives the birds toward them.

GRILLED QUAIL WITH SWEET BACON SAUCE

Makes: 2 servings   **Prep Time:** 15 minutes   **Cook Time:** 30 to 45 minutes

INGREDIENTS

- 2 whole quail breasts
- ¼ C. olive oil
- 1 tsp. garlic powder
- 1 tsp. dried cilantro
- 1 small onion
- 1 clove garlic
- 3 bacon strips
- 1 tsp. sherry vinegar
- 1½ tsp. honey
- ½ C. haricot verts or long French green beans*
- ½ tsp. dried cilantro
- Salt and pepper

* Frozen or canned green beans can be used in place of the haricot verts.

PREPARATION

Place the quail breasts in a medium bowl. Pour the olive oil over the quail and sprinkle with the garlic powder and cilantro; turn to coat both sides. Place the bowl in the refrigerator for 2 hours to marinate.

Meanwhile, prepare the sauce. Dice the onion and mince the garlic. In a medium skillet over medium-high heat, cook the bacon strips until tender. Remove the bacon to paper towels to drain but reserve 1 teaspoon of the bacon drippings in the pan. Crumble the bacon and return to the pan. Add the onion and garlic; sauté until the onions are translucent. Add the sherry vinegar and heat until almost all of the liquid has been absorbed. Stir in the honey and simmer for 1 additional minute. Add the haricot verts and cilantro. Season with salt and pepper to taste; reduce the heat to very low to keep the sauce warm while grilling the quail.

Prepare the grill to medium heat. Remove the quail breasts from the refrigerator and discard the marinade. Grill the quail breasts for 30 to 45 minutes or until the meat is cooked through.

To serve, place one grilled quail breast on each serving plate. Spoon a generous amount of the haricot verts and sauce over each serving.

★★★★ SPORTSMAN COOKING ★★★★

SIT STILL & GRILL

Grilling is a very popular method for preparing game birds for the table. To grill quail, place the cleaned bird on a rack about 8" above the heat. During grilling, use tongs to turn the quail often and be careful not to pierce the skin. Grill for about 45 minutes or until the meat is fork tender.

COOKING FISH & GAME

TERIYAKI PHEASANT

Makes: 4 servings   **Prep Time:** 15 minutes plus 4½ hours marinating   **Cook Time:** 1½ hours

INGREDIENTS

- 2 pheasants, cut into serving pieces
- ¼ C. salt
- 3 cloves garlic
- ¼ C. vegetable oil
- ½ C. sugar
- 2 tsp. ground ginger
- 1 C. dry white wine
- 1 C. soy sauce
- 1 tsp. dry mustard powder

PREPARATION

Once the pheasant is cut into serving pieces, place the pieces in a large bowl. Sprinkle salt over the pheasant pieces and add enough water to cover the pheasant. Cover the bowl and place in refrigerator for at least 4 hours.

Meanwhile, mince the garlic. In a small bowl, combine the garlic, vegetable oil, sugar, ginger, white wine, soy sauce and dry mustard powder; mix well.

Rinse the pheasant pieces under cool running water and place in a clean bowl. Pour the garlic marinade mixture over the pheasant and return to the refrigerator for 30 minutes to marinate.

Preheat the oven to 300°F. Remove the bowl from the refrigerator and transfer the pheasant pieces to a baking dish. Discard the marinade. Roast uncovered for 1½ to 2½ hours, or until fork-tender. Baste every 30 minutes with additional soy sauce.

★★★★ TWELVE-POINT FACT ★★★★

WILD WINGS

Meat from wild birds tends to be reddish in color, while farmed birds tend to have white flesh with yellow fat around the wing joints. Many believe that the meat from hens is more tender, while the meat from males tends to have more flavor.

SAVORY ROASTED PHEASANT

Makes: 4 servings   **Prep Time:** 10 to 15 minutes   **Cook Time:** 1 hour and 10 minutes

INGREDIENTS

- 2 pheasants, cut into serving pieces
- ¼ C. flour
- 1 tsp. salt
- 1 tsp. pepper
- Pinch of paprika
- 2 T. butter or margarine
- 2 medium onions
- ½ C. sweet vermouth
- 1 tsp. tomato paste
- ⅛ tsp. ground cinnamon
- 1 tsp. salt
- Pinch of pepper
- Butter or margarine

PREPARATION

Once the pheasant is cut into serving pieces, place the pieces in a large bowl. In a small bowl, combine the flour, salt, pepper and paprika; mix well. Pour the flour mixture over the pheasant pieces in the bowl and turn until all pieces are evenly dusted.

Preheat the oven to 350°F. In a large skillet over medium-high heat, melt the butter. Cook the pheasant pieces in the butter until evenly browned on all sides. Transfer the pheasant pieces to a roasting pan.

Dice the onions and add to the skillet over medium heat. Stir in the sweet vermouth, tomato paste, cinnamon, salt and a pinch of pepper. Sauté for about 2 minutes or until the onions are translucent and tender. Pour the sautéed onion mixture around the pheasant pieces in the roasting pan.

Dot pieces of butter over the pheasant and place the roasting pan in the oven. Roast for 1 hour or until the pheasant meat is tender.

To serve, arrange the roasted pheasant pieces in a serving dish. Spoon some of the sauce from the pan over the pheasant. If desired, arrange buttered toast triangles in the dish and garnish with sprigs of fresh parsley.

"When he was young, I told Dale Jr. that hunting and racing are a lot alike. Holding that steering wheel and holding that rifle both mean you better be responsible."

—— DALE EARNHARDT

QUAIL & GOAT CHEESE STUFFED CHILIES

Makes: 8 servings   **Prep Time:** 20 minutes   **Cook Time:** 45 minutes

INGREDIENTS

- 8 large Poblano chilies
- 4 green onions
- 2 cloves garlic
- 2 T. olive oil
- 8 whole quail breasts, cut into ¼" pieces
- 1 T. tequila
- ⅛ to ¼ tsp. dried cilantro
- 1 lb. goat cheese
- Salsa

PREPARATION

Start by roasting the chilies. Using long tongs, hold each pepper over a gas flame and turn until the skin of the pepper is evenly charred. Or, place the peppers on a baking sheet and roast under the broiler, turning to darken all sides but being careful not to burn. Transfer the peppers to a sealable plastic bag. Seal the bag and let the peppers steam. Wear rubber gloves to carefully peel the skin from the cooled chilies. Make an incision down the side of each of the chilies and remove all the seeds.

Preheat the oven to 350°F. Chop the white and green part of the green onions and mince the garlic. Heat the olive oil in a large skillet over medium-high heat. Sauté the green onions, garlic and quail until the onions are tender and the quail is browned.

Deglaze the skillet by stirring in the tequila; remove from heat. Once the ingredients are room temperature, stir in the cilantro and goat cheese; mix until evenly combined.

Carefully stuff the quail and goat cheese mixture into the roasted peppers. If desired, the peppers can be sewn closed using strips of blanched leeks and a needle. Place the peppers, stuffed side up, on a baking sheet and cover with aluminum foil. Bake in the oven for 40 minutes. Uncover and carefully turn the peppers so any liquids leak out. Return to the oven and roast uncovered for 5 additional minutes.

To serve, place a small pool of salsa on each serving plate; sprinkle with cilantro leaves. Place one stuffed pepper over the salsa on each plate.

★★★★ OPEN SEASON ★★★★

NUTRITIOUS & DELICIOUS

The meat of one quail has about 123 calories, 20 grams of protein and about 4.2 grams of total fat. Quail meat is an excellent source of iron, selenium and niacin, and a good source of zinc.

COOKING FISH & GAME

EASY CREAMED PHEASANT

Makes: 4 servings **Prep Time:** 10 minutes **Cook Time:** 1½ hours

INGREDIENTS

- ½ C. flour
- 2 whole pheasant breasts, cut into ¼" pieces
- ½ C. butter or margarine
- ¼ C. chopped onion
- Salt and pepper
- 2 C. sour cream
- ¼ C. chopped fresh parsley
- Toast or biscuits

PREPARATION

Preheat the oven to 350°F. Place the flour in a large shallow dish and dredge the pheasant pieces in the flour.

In a large skillet over medium-high heat, melt the butter. Add the coated pheasant pieces and onion to the skillet and sauté until the onions are softened. Sprinkle with salt and pepper. Once the onions are tender and the pheasant pieces are browned, transfer the mixture to a 9" square glass baking dish. Spread the sour cream over the pheasant and sprinkle with the chopped parsley. Cover the baking dish and bake for 1½ hours.

To serve, spoon the creamed pheasant mixture over toast or open-faced biscuits on each serving plate.

"Pheasant is the king of earthly poultry, as the primary of aquatic birds belongs to the swan. What more exquisite flesh can you eat?"

— OLIVIER DE SERRE

The **AMERICAN CLASSIC**

TIPS ABOUT FIELD DRESSING & MORE:

- If it's cool outside and you are close to home, you can wait to dress the bird until you get home. However, if it's hot outside and/or you are far from home, the turkey should be dressed in the field.

- After the bird is field dressed, you may want to consider how the turkey will be cooked. If the turkey will be roasted, smoked or deep fried whole, it is best to leave the skin on the turkey. If the turkey pieces will be fried or grilled, it is best to remove the skin from the bird.

- Some turkeys have more than 5,000 feathers. It is easiest to pluck a bird that has been dipped in very hot water (140°F is recommended).

- It is often easier to just remove the wing at the first joint rather than plucking the large primary wing feathers.

AMERICAN BIRD

There are four subspecies of the wild turkey native to the United States: Eastern, Osceola, Rio Grande and Merriam's. The Gould's subspecies and the Ocellated Turkey, which is its own species, live in parts of Mexico and Central America.

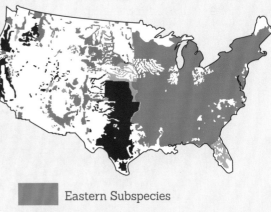

- Eastern Subspecies
- Osceola Subspecies
- Rio Grande Subspecies
- Merriam's Subspecies
- Inhabited by Hybridized Subspecies

Tail Feathers or Retrices

Back & Body Feathers

Snood

Major Caruncles

Breast Feathers

Beard

Wild Eastern Tom

Primary Wing Feathers

Spur

THE NATIONAL WILD TURKEY FEDERATION

ROASTED WILD TURKEY

Makes: 12 servings **Prep Time:** 20 minutes **Cook Time:** 5½ hours

INGREDIENTS

- ½ lb. bacon strips
- 1 medium onion
- 2 stalks celery
- ½ C. dry red wine
- 1 chicken bouillon cube
- 1 (6-oz.) pkg. turkey stuffing mix
- 1 (10- to 15-lb.) wild turkey
- ½ lb. bacon strips
- ½ C. dry red wine

PREPARATION

In a large skillet over medium-high heat, fry a half pound of bacon strips until crisp. Remove the bacon to paper towels to drain, reserving the bacon drippings in the skillet. Chop the onion and celery stalks and add to the skillet. Sauté until the onion begins to soften.

Stir the red wine, chicken bouillon cube and ½ cup water into the skillet with the onion and celery. Place the stuffing mix in a medium bowl. Pour the sautéed onion mixture and liquid from the skillet into the bowl; mix well. If the stuffing is too dry, add a little hot water and fluff with a fork. Crumble the cooked bacon and stir into the stuffing mix.

Preheat the oven to 300°F. Remove the giblets and neck from the turkey and rinse the turkey in cold water. Using paper towels, thoroughly pat dry both the outside and inside cavity of the turkey. Stuff the turkey with the stuffing mixture and stitch closed with kitchen twine or poultry pins.

Place the stuffed turkey in a roasting pan and drape another half pound of bacon strips over the turkey breast. Cover the roasting pan with a double layer of aluminum foil. Place the pan in the oven and roast for 4½ hours.

After 4½ hours, remove the foil and pour ½ cup red wine over the turkey. Return the pan to the oven and cook uncovered for an additional 45 minutes, basting every 15 minutes with the pan drippings. Remove the stuffing from the bird and place it in a baking dish. Continue to cook the stuffing in the oven to at least 165°F.

★★★★ OPEN SEASON ★★★★

TURKEY TURNAROUND

In the early 1900s, less than 30,000 wild turkeys remained in the United States and the bird was facing extinction. Fortunately, hunters, wildlife preservationists and conservation organizations intervened, causing the turkey population to rebound dramatically. Today, more than 7 million wild turkeys roam North America, with huntable populations in every state but Alaska.

THE NATIONAL WILD TURKEY FEDERATION

CAJUN DEEP-FRIED TURKEY

Makes: 12 servings **Prep Time:** 25 minutes **Cook Time:** 3 to 4 minutes per pound

INGREDIENTS

- ½ C. kosher salt
- 3 T. onion powder
- 3 T. pepper
- 3 T. white pepper
- 2 T. dried basil
- 2 tsp. crushed bay leaves
- 1 T. cayenne pepper
- 2 tsp. filé powder*
- 3 T. garlic powder
- 1½ T. paprika
- 1 (10- to 15-lb.) wild turkey
- 4 to 5 gallons peanut oil

A fried turkey is sure to be enjoyed by all your dinner guests, but make sure you take safety precautions when preparing this delicious meal. Measure the amount of oil you need carefully, keep your fryer away from flammable objects, and do not leave the fryer unattended.

PREPARATION

In a small bowl, combine the kosher salt, onion powder, pepper, white pepper, basil, bay leaves, cayenne pepper, filé powder, garlic powder and paprika; mix until well blended. For a 10-pound turkey, use half of the mixture as a rub; for a 15-pound turkey, use almost all of the rub. The remaining rub can be stored in an airtight jar for several months.

Remove the giblets and neck, and rinse the turkey with cold water. Using paper towels, thoroughly pat dry both the outside and inside cavity of the turkey.

Place the turkey in a large roasting pan and rub the seasoning mixture all over the inside and outside of the turkey. Cut the wing tips and small tail from the turkey. Cover the roasting pan and place in the refrigerator overnight.

Add the appropriate amount of peanut oil to a 7 to 10 gallon fryer pot. Set the fryer to medium-high setting and heat the oil to 375°F. It should take about 40 minutes to heat the oil. Meanwhile, place the turkey, neck down, in the turkey fryer basket or on the rack.

When the oil temperature reaches 375°F on a deep-fry thermometer, slowly lower the turkey into the oil. Immediately check the oil temperature and increase the flame so the temperature is maintained at 350°F. If the temperature drops below 340°, oil will begin to seep into the turkey. Fry the turkey for about 3 to 4 minutes per pound. Stay near the cooker so the heat can be regulated. Using a meat thermometer, check the temperature of the breast or thigh. When the breast has been cooked to 170°F or the thigh has been cooked to 180°F, carefully remove the basket and turn off the fryer. Allow the turkey to drain and rest for about 20 minutes before carving.

* Filé powder is an ingredient made from ground sassafras leaves. Filé powder is used in a lot of Creole cooking, often to thicken gumbo and give it a unique kick in flavor.

SETTING UP YOUR TREE STAND

Properly setting up your tree stand ensures a safe and successful hunt. Here are some things to keep in mind as you are setting up.

SAFETY FIRST. Use safety equipment like a safety harness and lineman's belt when hanging your tree stand. Tell someone where you are going before you leave, and bring a fully charged phone with you. Wear a good set of gloves to protect your hands during setup. Once your tree stand is up, use a lifeline to ensure you can get in and out of the stand safely.

USE THE RIGHT TOOLS. To set up your tree stand as quickly and efficiently as possible, you'll need the right tools. Bring a drill, a saw and a tree stand hanging device to help things go smoothly.

PACK THE RIGHT GEAR. Pack a pencil and paper so you can make notes about the area and the tree stand, especially if you're setting up during the offseason. Bring a map of the area to get a good picture of your hunting location. Bring a cooler with plenty of snacks to keep your energy high during setup, and a set of clean clothes for the trip home.

WEAR THE RIGHT CLOTHES. Wear a pair of cargo pants or something similar with a lot of pockets. You'll find the pockets incredibly useful for holding equipment as you work. Make sure you have good footwear, too. A sturdy pair of boots is the best choice.

PLAN AHEAD. Don't wait until the day of the hunt to set up equipment like gear hooks and your gun stand. Do it while you're setting up your tree stand. Clear a pathway to the stand to ensure you will leave as little scent on the ground as possible the day of the hunt. Mark the pathway with florescent tape or something similar so you can easily find your way in the dark.

Once you have set up your tree stand properly, you'll have nothing to worry about the day of the hunt except bagging the biggest catch possible.

GRILLED SESAME TURKEY BREAST

Makes: 4 servings   **Prep Time:** 10 minutes plus 8 hours marinating   **Cook Time:** 1½ hours

INGREDIENTS

- ➤ 1 whole wild turkey breast
- ➤ 1 C. soy sauce
- ➤ 1 C. brown sugar
- ➤ ½ C. sesame oil
- ➤ ½ C. sesame seeds
- ➤ 2 T. pepper
- ➤ 10 green onions, minced
- ➤ 10 cloves garlic, minced
- ➤ 1 T. fresh grated gingerroot
- ➤ 2 T. butter or margarine, melted

PREPARATION

The turkey breast can either be deboned or not. Cut the turkey breast into serving size pieces across the grain.

In a medium bowl, combine the soy sauce, brown sugar, sesame oil, sesame seeds, pepper, green onions, garlic, gingerroot and melted butter; mix well. Add the turkey pieces to the bowl, turning until evenly coated. Place the bowl in the refrigerator for 8 hours or overnight to marinate. (If you wish to baste the turkey meat while grilling, set aside and refrigerate ½ to ¾ cup of the marinade before combining the rest of the marinade with the turkey breast pieces.)

Preheat the grill to medium-high heat. Remove the bowl from the refrigerator and discard the marinade. Place the turkey pieces on the grill over indirect heat. Though this will take longer to cook, the meat won't dry out as easily over indirect heat. Grill the turkey pieces for about 1½ hours or until cooked through, basting every 30 minutes with the reserved marinade, if desired. Check for doneness after 45 minutes. The meat will be done when it reaches an internal temperature of 170°F as measured on a meat thermometer.

★★★★ HUNTSMAN'S HINT ★★★★

COLORLESS CAMO

Without proper care, camouflage clothing can lose its color after a few washings. To protect your camo from fading, turn the garments inside out before washing. Hand washing the clothing will help maintain a long color life. To do this, fill a five-gallon bucket with cold water. Mix in ½ cup of baking soda and slosh the clothing up and down a few times. Let the clothing sit in the mixture for 8 hours or overnight. Wring and shake out the garments before hanging them to dry. If using a washing machine, choose the cold water setting and wash in the delicate cycle; hang clothing to air-dry.

CHICKEN FRIED WILD TURKEY BREAST

Makes: 4 servings   **Prep Time:** 15 minutes   **Cook Time:** 10 to 15 minutes

INGREDIENTS

- 1 whole wild turkey breast
- 1 (16-oz.) bottle Italian dressing
- ½ tsp. lemon pepper
- ¼ tsp. liquid smoke flavoring
- 2 eggs
- 2 C. milk
- 2 C. flour
- ¼ tsp. salt
- ¼ tsp. pepper
- Peanut or vegetable oil
- 2 T. flour
- 2 T. butter or margarine, melted
- Salt and pepper
- 1 C. milk

PREPARATION

Debone the turkey breast and cut the meat into strips across the grain. In a medium bowl, combine the Italian dressing, lemon pepper and liquid smoke flavoring; mix well. Add the turkey strips to the bowl, turning until evenly coated. Place the bowl in the refrigerator for 8 hours or overnight to marinate.

Beat the eggs in a small bowl. Add 2 cups of milk and whisk together. In a separate bowl, combine the 2 cups of flour, salt and pepper; mix well. Remove the turkey strips from the refrigerator and discard the marinade. Dip the marinated turkey strips first into the egg mixture and then into the flour mixture.

Heat ¼" to ½" oil in a large skillet over medium-high heat. Once the oil is hot, carefully place the coated turkey strips in the skillet and fry until golden brown, turning once. Remove the turkey strips to paper towels to drain.

To prepare the gravy, add 2 tablespoons of flour to the remaining oil and drippings in the skillet. Whisk in the melted butter; season with a pinch of salt and pepper. Slowly whisk in 1 cup milk, stirring constantly until the gravy is thick.

To serve, place fried turkey strips on serving plates. Drizzle gravy over turkey or serve gravy on the side.

★★★★ **OPEN SEASON** ★★★★

PECKING ORDER

Picking out the dominant tom in a flock of wild turkeys can sometimes be difficult. The tom is often the biggest and/or oldest gobbler and can be identified by the way he acts. The dominant tom with a long beard will do almost all or most of the strutting within the flock. The other gobblers around the dominant bird may strut, but for a shorter amount of time or not as fully fanned. Also, the dominant tom may attack other gobblers or turn in their direction, causing them to move or break their strut.

THE NATIONAL WILD TURKEY FEDERATION

DEEP-DISH TURKEY PIE

Makes: 6 to 8 servings   **Prep Time:** 15 minutes   **Cook Time:** 45 to 50 minutes

INGREDIENTS

- 6 medium potatoes
- 6 medium carrots
- 1 small onion
- ½ green bell pepper
- 2 T. butter or margarine
- 1 (10¾-oz.) can cream of chicken soup
- 3 C. diced cooked wild turkey meat
- 1½ C. flour
- 2 tsp. baking powder
- ½ tsp. salt
- ¼ C. butter or margarine
- ½ C. milk

PREPARATION

Clean and dice the potatoes and carrots. In a large saucepan or pot over medium-high heat, place the potatoes and carrots. Add enough water to cover the vegetables. Bring the water to a boil, reduce heat to medium-low, cover the saucepan and simmer until the potatoes and carrots are tender, about 15 to 20 minutes. Remove from the heat and drain the water from the saucepan, reserving 1 cup of the liquid.

Preheat the oven to 425°F. Chop the onion and half of the green bell pepper. In a medium skillet, sauté the onion and green pepper in the butter. Heat, stirring often, until the onion is translucent and tender.

In a small bowl, combine the reserved 1 cup cooking liquid and the cream of chicken soup.

In a 2-quart casserole dish, place the sautéed onions and peppers, cooked carrots and potatoes, and the cooked turkey. Pour the soup mixture over top and mix until all ingredients are well combined. Bake for 15 minutes.

Meanwhile, prepare the biscuits. In a medium bowl, combine the flour, baking powder and salt. Using a pastry blender, cut in ¼ cup of butter until the mixture is crumbly. Add the milk and mix well. Knead the dough lightly on a floured surface. Roll out the dough and cut into circles using a 2" biscuit cutter. Carefully remove the casserole dish from the oven and arrange the biscuits over the turkey mixture. Brush the biscuits with a little milk and return to the oven for an additional 15 minutes.

★★★★ TWELVE-POINT FACT ★★★★

THE TURKEY TERM

The turkey gained its name after Spanish explorers brought the native American bird back to Europe more than 400 years ago. The English thought the bird was the same as the African Guinea fowl they imported from Guinea through the Middle Eastern country of Turkey, which they named "turkey". They mistakenly gave the American bird the same name.

WHITE TURKEY CHILI

Makes: 10 to 12 servings   **Prep Time:** 15 minutes   **Cook Time:** 1 hour

INGREDIENTS

- 1 whole wild turkey breast
- 1 large onion
- 2 to 3 T. butter or margarine
- 3 (15-oz.) cans white Northern beans
- 1 (11-oz.) can white corn
- 2 (4-oz.) cans chopped green chilies
- 2 (10½-oz.) cans chicken broth
- ¼ tsp. onion powder
- ⅛ tsp. garlic powder
- ¼ tsp. celery salt
- ¼ tsp. paprika
- ½ tsp. dried parsley flakes
- 1 T. ground cumin
- ⅛ tsp. ground cloves
- ¼ tsp. dried oregano
- Salt and pepper
- 1 C. shredded Monterey Jack cheese

PREPARATION

Debone and chop the turkey breasts into ¼" to ½" pieces. Dice the onion. Place the butter in a large soup pot over medium-high heat. Sauté the turkey meat and onion in the butter for 5 minutes or until the turkey is browned and the onions are translucent and tender.

Reduce the heat to medium-low and add 1 cup water. Drain the Northern beans, white corn and green chilies; add the beans, corn and chilies to the soup pot. Stir in the chicken broth, onion powder, garlic powder, celery salt, paprika, parsley flakes, cumin, ground cloves and oregano. Season with salt and pepper to taste. Cover the pot and let simmer for 1 hour.

To serve, ladle the soup into bowls. Top each serving with some shredded Monterey Jack cheese.

★★★★ SPORTSMAN COOKING ★★★★

OIL RESERVE

To determine the correct amount of oil to use in a turkey fryer, place the turkey in the fryer (before adding any seasonings) and fill the pot with water until the turkey is covered. Remove the turkey and measure the amount of water in the fryer. Use a corresponding amount of oil when frying the turkey. Dry the fryer thoroughly of all water before adding oil or storing.

Popular **WATER FOWL**

Many types of ducks and geese share the same habitats, are hunted by the same methods, and have overlapping or identical hunting seasons. Therefore, it is not uncommon for a waterfowl hunter to take several types of ducks and geese in the same outing.

Most ducks have a wide flat beak adapted for dredging food such as insects, fish, aquatic plants, worms and small amphibians. Because of their similar appearance, ducks are sometimes confused with several types of unrelated water birds, such as loons, grebes, gallinules and coots.

Geese are medium to large birds that are always associated with water to some degree. Most species are strongly migratory as wild birds, breeding in the far north and wintering much farther south. All geese eat a largely vegetarian diet, but domesticated geese will try out most novel food items for edibility. Geese usually mate for life, and both parents protect the nest of their young, resulting in a higher survival rate for goslings than ducklings.

Mallard Duck (drake)

Canada Goose

TIPS FOR FIELD DRESSING & MORE:

- Field dress the bird immediately. Remove the entrails and take care not to break the bladder. Wipe the body cavity thoroughly with a dry cloth, as any moisture could cause spreading of bacteria.

- Prop the body cavity open with a small stick to allow air to circulate and cool the body heat. Bring a cooler to transport the bird.

- Finish dressing the bird at home. A fully dressed duck can be aged safely by refrigerating for three or four days, which will tenderize the meat and help develop flavor.

- Experts recommend that ducks and geese be plucked rather than skinned because the skin helps retain flavor and moisture during cooking. Dry pluck as many feathers as possible. Use a paraffin treatment to remove pin feathers and down.

- Do not freeze birds without plucking and cleaning them first. Thaw a frozen duck or goose by placing it in the refrigerator for 12 to 18 hours. This slow thaw will tenderize the meat and help prevent growth of bacteria.

- Use a high acid marinade for fish-eating ducks (those with pointed or serrated bills). Lemon or lime juice, vinegar, wine or buttermilk work well. Soak older ducks and geese for 4 to 12 hours in the refrigerator in a solution of ½ teaspoon salt and 1 tablespoon vinegar per quart of cold water.

★★★★ OPEN SEASON ★★★★

DUCK STAMP

By the turn of the century, loss of habitat and commercial hunting lead to a decline in the duck and goose populations of North America. The dawn of the modern conservation movement was marked by the Lacey Act of 1900, outlawing the transport of poached game across state lines. At the urging of editorial cartoonist and conservationist J. N. "Ding" Darling, the US government passed the Migratory Bird Hunting Stamp Act, better known as the Federal Duck Stamp Act, in 1934. This program required hunters to purchase a special stamp, in addition to a regular hunting license, to hunt migratory waterfowl. Revenues from this program provided major funding for conservation for many decades and funded the purchase of 4.5 million acres of National Wildlife Refuge land. The Duck Stamp Act has been described as "one of the most successful conservation programs ever devised."

BARBECUED WILD DUCK

Makes: 4 servings   **Prep Time:** 15 minutes plus 12 hours soaking and marinating
Cook Time: 1 hour to 1 hour and 20 minutes

INGREDIENTS

- ➤ 2 whole ducks
- ➤ 1 clove garlic
- ➤ ½ C. lemon juice
- ➤ 1½ C. vegetable oil
- ➤ ½ tsp. dried thyme
- ➤ ½ tsp. celery seed
- ➤ 1½ C. tomato juice
- ➤ ¼ C. vinegar
- ➤ ½ C. vegetable oil
- ➤ 1 T. minced onion
- ➤ ½ tsp. salt
- ➤ 1 tsp. Worcestershire sauce
- ➤ 1 T. prepared mustard
- ➤ ⅛ tsp. cayenne pepper
- ➤ ½ tsp. chili powder
- ➤ ¼ tsp. paprika
- ➤ ½ tsp. sugar
- ➤ Hot pepper sauce

PREPARATION

Soak each plucked and cleaned duck in a solution of 1 quart water and 1 tablespoon baking soda for 2 to 3 hours. Rinse the ducks thoroughly and drain. Pat the ducks dry with paper towels.

Mince the garlic. In a medium bowl, combine the lemon juice, vegetable oil, thyme, celery seed and half of the garlic. Place the dry ducks in a 9 x 13" baking dish and pour the marinade mixture over the ducks. Place the baking dish in the refrigerator for 10 to 12 hours to marinate.

Preheat the oven to 350°F. Remove the baking dish from the refrigerator and transfer the ducks to a roasting pan. Discard the marinade. Roast uncovered for 20 minutes.

Meanwhile, prepare the sauce. In a large saucepan over medium heat, combine the tomato juice, vinegar and vegetable oil. Mix in the onion, salt, Worcestershire sauce, mustard, cayenne pepper, chili powder, paprika and sugar. Add a few drops of hot pepper sauce. Mix well and bring to a boil. Reduce heat and let simmer for 10 minutes.

After the 20 minutes of roasting time, remove the roasting pan from the oven. Pour half of the barbecue sauce over and around the ducks. Cover the roasting pan and return to the oven to cook for 20 minutes per pound of duck.

To serve, place the roasted ducks on a platter. Drizzle the remaining hot barbecue sauce over the ducks or serve the sauce on the side.

"The perils of duck hunting are great—especially for the duck."

— WALTER CRONKITE

ROAST DUCK WITH ORANGE SAUCE

Makes: 2 servings   **Prep Time:** 15 to 20 minutes plus 2 hours soaking   **Cook Time:** 40 to 60 minutes

INGREDIENTS

- 1 whole duck
- Salt and pepper
- 2 apples
- 1 large onion
- 1 large carrot
- 2 stalks celery
- 6 bacon strips
- 2 oranges
- 1½ C. beef broth, divided
- ¼ C. butter or margarine
- ¼ C. flour
- ½ tsp. salt
- ⅛ tsp. cayenne pepper
- 1 lemon
- 2 T. sherry wine
- 1 T. currant jelly

PREPARATION

Soak the plucked and cleaned duck in a solution of 1 quart water and 1 tablespoon baking soda for 2 to 3 hours. Rinse the duck thoroughly and pat dry with paper towels.

Preheat the oven to 350°F. Sprinkle the duck with salt and pepper. Coarsely chop the apples, onion, carrot and celery. Stuff the duck with the chopped fruit and vegetables and truss with kitchen twine, or close the opening with poultry pins. Arrange the stuffed duck in a roasting pan. Drape the strips of bacon over the duck.

Place the roasting pan in the oven and bake uncovered for 15 to 20 minutes per pound. Baste the duck every 15 minutes with juices from the bottom of the pan.

Meanwhile, prepare the sauce. Finely slice or grate the peel of one orange. In a medium saucepan over medium heat, bring ½ cup water to a simmer. Stir in the orange peel and 1 cup of beef broth. In a large saucepan over medium-high heat, melt the butter. Stir in the flour, salt and cayenne pepper. Heat until the mixture is just lightly browned and add the remaining ½ cup beef broth. Gradually squeeze in the juice of one lemon and both oranges. Next, mix in the simmering orange peel mixture; bring to a boil, then reduce heat to hold the sauce at a light simmer. Just before serving, stir in the sherry and currant jelly; heat and stir until the jelly melts.

To serve, place the roasted duck on a platter. Remove the apple, onion, carrot and celery pieces from the ducks and discard. Carve the duck meat into slices and serve with orange sauce on the side.

DUCK & SHRIMP GUMBO

Makes: 6 to 8 servings   **Prep Time:** 20 minutes   **Cook Time:** 1½ to 2 hours

INGREDIENTS

- 2 ducks, cut into serving pieces
- 1 T. vegetable oil
- ½ C. flour
- 2 medium onions
- 2 stalks celery
- 1 large red bell pepper
- 1 large green bell pepper
- 4 bay leaves
- 2 tsp. salt
- 6 C. chicken broth
- 6 green onions
- 1 lb. medium shrimp, peeled and deveined
- ¼ tsp. cayenne pepper

Bumpers are a great way to train your retriever and keep him in form during the off-season. As hunting season approaches, though, be sure to reintroduce him to birds using frozen or live game.

PREPARATION

Clean the duck pieces and pat dry with paper towels. Prick the skin of the duck all over with the tip of a sharp knife.

In a large heavy pot over medium-high heat, heat the vegetable oil. Add the duck pieces in batches and brown on all sides. Transfer the browned duck pieces to a bowl and drain all but ¼ cup of the pan drippings. Return the pot to medium-low heat. Stir the flour into the drippings in the pan. Heat for about 10 minutes, stirring often, until the roux is well-browned like the color of peanut butter.

Meanwhile, chop the onions, celery and peppers. Stir the onions, celery, peppers, bay leaves and salt into the pot. Heat, stirring occasionally, until the vegetables are tender but still crisp. Stir in 4 cups of water, the chicken broth and the browned duck pieces. Bring the soup to a boil, reduce the heat and let simmer until the duck is tender, about 1¼ to 1½ hours.

Remove the soup from the heat. Transfer the duck pieces to a cutting board and shred the meat into large pieces, discarding any bones and skin. Skim any fat from the surface of the soup. Return the duck meat to the gumbo and bring to a boil. Meanwhile, chop the green onion stems. Reduce the soup to a simmer and stir in the green onions, shrimp and cayenne pepper. Heat for about 2 minutes. Remove and discard the bay leaves before serving.

HOLIDAY GOOSE

Makes: 6 to 8 servings   **Prep Time:** 40 minutes to 1 hour   **Cook Time:** 15 to 20 minutes per pound

INGREDIENTS

- 1 whole wild goose
- 1 large onion
- 2 Jonathan apples
- 10 C. cornbread crumbs
- 1 tsp. salt
- 1 tsp. pepper
- ½ tsp. dried sage
- ¼ tsp. garlic powder
- 2 T. butter or margarine, softened
- 2 T. flour

PREPARATION

Pluck and clean the goose, leaving the skin intact. Reserve the giblets. Boil the neck and giblets until tender; remove any skin and chop fine. Wipe the goose, inside and out, with a damp cloth. Prick the skin every inch with a sharp knife or fork.

Preheat the oven to 350°F. Finely chop the onion and dice the apples. In a medium bowl, combine the chopped giblets, onion, apples and cornbread crumbs. Add the salt, pepper, sage and garlic powder. Add ¼ cup of water and mix together until well combined. Stuff the goose with the cornbread stuffing and truss with kitchen twine, or close the opening with poultry pins.

Place the goose in a roasting pan. Spread the softened butter over the goose and sprinkle with the flour. Place the roasting pan in the oven. Roast for 15 to 20 minutes per pound. Baste every 30 minutes with juices from the pan.

To serve, place the goose on a platter. Remove the stuffing from the goose and transfer to a baking dish. If the stuffing registers below 165°F on a meat thermometer, return to the oven until the temperature of the stuffing reaches at least 165°F. Carve the goose and serve with the cornbread stuffing on the side.

★★★★ SPORTSMAN COOKING ★★★★

DARK MEAT

Goose consists of entirely dark meat, which has been likened to well-done roast beef. While the meat is very lean (7 grams of fat and 160 calories per 3.6 ounces of skinless meat), there is a great deal of fat between the skin and the meat. Before roasting, the skin should be pricked every inch to release the fat.

U.S. DEPARTMENT OF AGRICULTURE

GOOSE BREAST A L'ORANGE

Makes: 2 to 4 servings   **Prep Time:** 15 to 20 minutes   **Cook Time:** 20 to 30 minutes

INGREDIENTS

- ½ C. frozen orange juice concentrate
- 1 T. minced fresh gingerroot
- 2 T. Grand Marnier liqueur
- 1 T. soy sauce
- ½ C. duck or chicken broth
- 2 T. brown sugar
- 2 T. currant jelly
- 2 T. butter or margarine
- Salt and pepper
- 1 T. cornstarch
- 2 whole wild goose breasts
- 2 T. steak seasoning

PREPARATION

In a medium saucepan over medium heat, combine the orange juice concentrate, gingerroot, liqueur, soy sauce and broth. Heat, stirring occasionally, until the liquid is reduced and becomes slightly syrupy. Stir in the brown sugar and jelly. Turn off the heat and mix in the butter and a pinch of salt and pepper. In a small glass, combine the cornstarch with 2 tablespoons water; mix well. Stir the cornstarch mixture into the sauce. The sauce will thicken as it sits.

Preheat an outdoor grill to medium-high heat. Debone and clean the goose breasts; pat dry with paper towels. Generously season both sides of the breasts with steak seasoning. Pound the breasts slightly with a meat mallet for even thickness. Grill the breasts until the meat is seared on both sides and cooked through to medium-rare or medium.

To serve, place the breasts on a platter and let them rest a few minutes before slicing. Carve the meat into ½" thick slices. Place the meat slices on serving plates and spoon a generous amount of the warmed orange sauce over each serving.

★★★★ **TWELVE-POINT FACT** ★★★★

OH CANADA

With all those V-formations flying overhead, and unpleasant droppings left behind on park benches and golf courses, it is hard to believe that the Canada Goose was once an uncommon bird. In fact, some subspecies of the giant Canada Goose were considered extinct until a few remnant populations were discovered in the early 1960s. Improved game management practices and extensive re-introduction programs have successfully restored today's Canada Goose population.

BROILED BREAST OF WILD GOOSE

Makes: 2 to 4 servings   **Prep Time:** 15 minutes plus 8 hours marinating   **Cook Time:** 20 to 25 minutes

INGREDIENTS

- ➤ 2 whole wild goose breasts
- ➤ 1 T. minced onion
- ➤ ¼ C. finely shredded carrots
- ➤ 2 bay leaves
- ➤ ½ tsp. dried marjoram
- ➤ 1 tsp. dried sage
- ➤ 1 tsp. salt
- ➤ ½ tsp. pepper
- ➤ 2 C. white wine

PREPARATION

Debone and clean the goose breasts; pat dry with a paper towel. Place the breasts in a 9 x 13" glass baking dish.

In a medium bowl, combine the onion, carrots, bay leaves, marjoram, sage, salt, pepper and white wine; mix well. Pour the mixture over the goose breasts, turning the breasts to coat both sides. Place the baking dish in the refrigerator for 8 hours to marinate. Turn the breasts over every 2 hours.

Preheat the oven broiler. Remove the baking dish from the refrigerator and transfer the goose breasts to a metal rack placed over a baking sheet. Discard the marinade. Broil uncovered for 11 minutes. Turn the breasts over and broil for an additional 11 minutes or until the meat is cooked through.

★★★★ OPEN SEASON ★★★★

AMAZING MIGRATION

The annual migrations that birds make between their breeding and wintering grounds are one of the wonders of our natural world. Migrating birds, especially waterfowl, follow broad but well-defined migration routes called flyways or migration corridors. The four primary vertical corridors in North America are the Atlantic, Mississippi, Central and Pacific flyways. Snow Geese breed in the Artic Tundra and winter in south and southwest America. These geese make an annual round trip journey of more than 5,000 miles at speeds of 50 mph or more. In Asia, the Bar-headed Geese regularly migrate over the Himalayan Mountains, even over Mt. Everest at an altitude of 30,750 feet, where the air is thin and the temperature drops to -60°F.

Flavorful **SMALL GAME**

TIPS FOR FIELD DRESSING & MORE:

- Field dress the rabbit immediately, and wash all knives several times during field dressing with clean water.
- Remove the head and feet, cutting at the ankles.

Cottontail

Brown Hare

Black-tailed Jack Rabbit

- Holding the rabbit by the back skin, make a cut through the skin and over the back, but not into the meat. Peel back the skin in both directions, taking care not to let the fur or hide touch the carcass. Peel away all of the skin, including the tail.
- Remove the entrails, then cool and rinse the carcass as quickly as possible. Pat the carcass dry with a cloth or paper towels.
- If you prefer to dress the rabbit at home, the fur, feet and head can be removed later, but the entrails should be removed quickly after the kill. Make an incision under the rabbit's sternum and up to the neck, being careful not to cut so deep as to puncture the organs. Reach inside and remove the entrails.
- Tularemia, or rabbit fever, is a decreasing but serious disease that attacks the internal organs of a rabbit. Humans can be infected with this disease through the handling of an infected animal. Hunters are at a higher risk because of the potential of inhaling the bacteria during the skinning process. Always carefully inspect the liver of a rabbit for spotting (often white or yellow spotting), which can indicate tularemia. If you even suspect you see spots, discard the carcass immediately.

SOUTHWESTERN RABBIT

Makes: 4 servings **Prep Time:** 15 to 20 minutes **Cook Time:** 1 hour and 15 minutes

INGREDIENTS

- ½ C. vegetable oil
- 1 rabbit, cut into serving pieces
- 1 small onion
- 3 stalks celery
- ½ small green bell pepper
- 2 T. vegetable oil
- 1 T. chili powder
- 1 C. ketchup
- 2 T. brown sugar
- 2 T. Worcestershire sauce
- 1 tsp. salt

PREPARATION

Place ½ cup of vegetable oil in a large skillet over medium-high heat. Once the oil is hot, brown the rabbit pieces on all sides. Transfer the browned rabbit pieces to a 9 x 13" glass baking dish.

Preheat the oven to 350°F. Chop the onion, celery and half of the green pepper. In the same skillet, add another 2 tablespoons of vegetable oil. Stir in the onion, celery and green bell pepper. Add the chili powder, ketchup, brown sugar, Worcestershire sauce, salt and 1 cup water. Mix well and bring to a boil. Pour the sauce over the rabbit pieces in the baking dish.

Place the baking dish in the oven. Bake uncovered for 30 minutes. Turn the rabbit pieces over and bake for an additional 30 minutes or until the rabbit is tender.

★★★★ HUNTSMAN'S HINT ★★★★

RABBIT WHEREABOUTS

Hunting for rabbits requires knowledge of rabbit behavior under varying weather conditions. A good time for rabbit sighting is on the first warm day after a cold spell when rabbits can be found in open fields soaking up the sunlight. However, on a cold or windy day, rabbits will tend to hide in thick tangles of vines, briars, overgrown brush and tall grasses.

RABBIT IN CREAM SAUCE

Makes: 4 servings   **Prep Time:** 15 minutes   **Cook Time:** 1 hour and 15 minutes

INGREDIENTS

- 1 rabbit, cut into serving pieces
- Salt
- ½ C. flour
- 2 T. vegetable oil
- 2 medium onions
- 2 slices lemon
- ½ tsp. dried oregano
- 1 bay leaf
- ¼ tsp. pepper
- 3 T. red wine vinegar
- 1 T. butter or margarine
- 1½ T. flour
- 2 C. sour cream
- ½ tsp. sugar

PREPARATION

Season the rabbit pieces with salt and dredge in flour. Place the vegetable oil in a large skillet over medium-high heat. Once the oil is hot, brown the rabbit pieces on all sides.

Chop the onions. Add the onions, lemon slices, oregano, bay leaf and pepper to the skillet. Add the red wine vinegar and simmer, stirring often, until the rabbit is tender, about 50 to 60 minutes.

Remove the rabbit pieces to a plate and keep warm. Add the butter and flour to the skillet. Mix into a roux, then stir in the sour cream and sugar. Bring to a light simmer and remove the bay leaf. If the sauce is too thick, add a little water.

To serve, place the rabbit pieces on serving plates and drizzle with the cream sauce or serve with boiled potatoes and sauce on the side.

★★★★ TWELVE-POINT FACT ★★★★

THE COMMON COTTONTAIL

The most common type of wild rabbit is the Eastern Cottontail. This species ranges from southern Canada through the United States and into northern South America. The Eastern Cottontail lives in a variety of habitats, including tropical, temperate hardwood and northern forests, grasslands, swamps, deserts, fields and farms. Most of these species have tails that are brown above and white below, resembling a cotton ball.

RABBIT FAJITAS

Makes: 2 to 4 servings   **Prep Time:** 15 minutes   **Cook Time:** 30 minutes

INGREDIENTS

- 1 rabbit, cut into serving pieces
- Salt
- 2 T. olive oil
- 2 red bell peppers
- 1 large onion
- 2 cloves garlic
- 2 T. olive oil
- 1 tsp. salt
- Fajita-size tortillas
- Sour cream
- Salsa

PREPARATION

Season the rabbit pieces with salt. Place the olive oil in a large skillet over medium-high heat. Once the oil is hot, brown the rabbit pieces on all sides. Continue to heat until the rabbit meat is cooked through. Remove the cooked rabbit pieces to a plate to cool.

Meanwhile, cut the red peppers into thin slices. Chop the onion and mince the garlic. Once the rabbit meat has cooled slightly, pull the meat from the bone and shred. Place another 2 tablespoons of olive oil in the skillet. Place the rabbit meat, pepper slices, onion and garlic in the skillet. Sprinkle the salt over top and sauté until the vegetables are tender.

To serve, spoon desired amount of the rabbit meat and vegetables onto each fajita tortilla. Top each with a dollop of sour cream and salsa. Roll up the fajitas and serve.

"We have been God-like in our planned breeding of our domesticated plants and animals, but we have been rabbit-like in our unplanned breeding of ourselves."

— ARNOLD TOYNBEE

MOREL MUSHROOMS

In addition to wild game and fish, nature provides many other types of natural foods, such as mushrooms, wild rice and berries. Morel mushrooms are a favorite find for many wildlife enthusiasts.

The United States morel season typically runs from early- or mid-April through mid-June. Depending on your geographical location, your local morel season could be within one or two weeks of this range. Once you hear of someone finding morels in your area, it is time to get out there and start hunting!

BATH TIME

After gathering your morels and returning home, here are some basic suggestions for cleaning the mushrooms:

- Slice the morels lengthwise into halves.
- Rinse the morels under cold water to remove any loose dirt or bugs.
- Fill the sink with cold water and add 1 scant teaspoon of salt.
- Drop the morels into the cold water and let them soak for no longer than 1 hour.
- Place the morels on a cotton cloth to drain.
- Store in a refrigerator, covered with soaked paper towels, and drain water as needed.

BASIC FRIED MORELS

Makes: 2 servings   **Prep Time:** 10 minutes   **Cook Time:** 10 minutes

INGREDIENTS

- 10 to 12 morel mushrooms
- 1 sleeve round butter crackers
- 2 eggs
- ¼ C. butter or margarine

PREPARATION

Clean, soak and set the morels on a cotton cloth to drain any water.

Finely crush the butter crackers into a bowl. Beat the eggs in a separate bowl. Dip each morel first into the egg and then into the crackers, turning to coat all sides.

Heat the butter in a large skillet over medium-high heat. Once the butter is melted and hot, fry the morels until golden brown, turning a few times. Drain the morels on paper towels before serving.

★★★★ SPORTSMAN COOKING ★★★★

A DEAD GIVEAWAY

Morel hunters often find a goldmine of grey morels near dead elm trees. Most often, the best searching spots are areas with elm trees that have died within the past year or two (with their bark still attached to the limbs and trunk). Yellow morels are attracted to sunlight and can usually be found on south-facing slopes in the deep woods, or areas in the heart of the forest floor that receive a lot of sunlight.

Index

ACQUISITION EDITOR:
Peg Couch

ASSISTANT EDITOR:
Colleen Dorsey

COVER AND LAYOUT DESIGNER:
Jason Deller

EDITOR:
Katie Weeber

PROOFREADER:
Lynda Jo Runkle

INDEXER
Jay Kreider

Lurecraft
ISBN 978-1-56523-780-3 **$19.99**

Cooking for the Man Cave
ISBN 978-1-56523-740-7 **$14.99**

Grilling Gone Wild
ISBN 978-1-56523-725-4 **$14.95**

Easy Campfire Cooking
ISBN 978-1-56523-724-7 **$12.95**

The Paddling Chef
ISBN 978-1-56523-714-8 **$16.95**

**Camp Cooking:
The Black Feather Guide**
ISBN 978-1-56523-644-8 **$19.95**

Edible Party Bouquets
ISBN 978-1-56523-723-0 **$14.95**

Spiked Desserts
ISBN 978-1-56523-722-3 **$14.95**

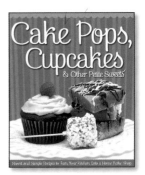

**Cake Pops, Cupcakes &
Other Petite Sweets**
ISBN 978-1-56523-739-1 **$14.99**